Ivy Global

ISEE UPPER LEVEL TESTS

1ST EDITION

IVY GLOBAL, NEW YORK

This publication was written and edited by the team at Ivy Global.

Editors: Corwin Henville and Laurel Perkins
Layout Editor: Sacha Azor
Contributors: Sarah Atkins, Ali Candib, Tamara Jordan, Nathan Létourneau, Sarah Pike, and Julia Romanski
Producers: Lloyd Min and Junho Suh

About Ivy Global

Ivy Global is a pioneering education company that provides a wide range of educational services.

E-mail: info@ivyglobal.com
Website: http://www.ivyglobal.com

CONTENTS

INTRODUCTION

CHAPTER 1

HOW TO USE THIS BOOK

SECTION 1

Welcome, students and parents! This book is intended for students practicing for the Upper Level Independent School Entrance Exam (ISEE). For students applying to many top private and independent schools in North America, the ISEE is a crucial and sometimes daunting step in the admissions process. By exposing you to the format of the ISEE, Ivy Global will help you build your confidence and maximize your score on this important exam.

This book is right for you if:

- you are applying to a private or independent school that requires the ISEE for admission
- you will be in Grades 8-11 when you take the ISEE
- you would like to practice for the ISEE exam using full-length practice tests under simulated testing conditions
- you are a parent, family member, or tutor looking for new ways to help your Upper Level ISEE student

We know that no two students are exactly alike—each student brings a unique combination of personal strengths and weaknesses to his or her test preparation. For this reason, we've tailored our preparation materials to help students with a specific subject area or goal.

Ivy Global's *ISEE English* includes the best strategies for the ISEE Verbal Reasoning and Reading Comprehension sections, plus a step-by-step approach to the Essay section and a thorough vocabulary and writing skills review.

Ivy Global's *ISEE Math* includes the best strategies for the ISEE Quantitative Reasoning and Mathematics Achievement sections, plus thorough review and practice for all of the math concepts tested at each level.

Ivy Global's products are available for purchase at ivyglobal.com/products or amazon.com.

This book includes:

- an up-to-date introduction to the ISEE's administration, format, and scoring practices
- instructions for taking a full-length practice test for the ISEE under simulated testing conditions
- 2 full-length practice tests for the ISEE Upper Level
- detailed scoring instructions for the exam

To make the best use of this book, take time to assess your strengths and weaknesses after you have worked through an exam. Then, spend some time reviewing the concepts you found challenging before you test yourself again.

To get started, continue reading for an overview of the ISEE. Good luck in this exciting new step for your education!

ABOUT THE ISEE

SECTION 2

The **ISEE (Independent School Entrance Exam)** is a standardized test administered to students in grades 1-11 to help determine placement into certain private and independent schools. Many secondary schools worldwide use the ISEE as an integral part of their admissions process. The ISEE is owned and published by the Educational Records Bureau.

You will register for one of four ISEE tests, depending on your grade level:

- The **Primary Level** exam is for students currently in grades 1-3.
- The **Lower Level** exam is for students currently in grades 4-5.
- The **Middle Level** exam is for students currently in grades 6-7.
- The **Upper Level** exam is for students currently in grades 8-11.

The Primary Level exam is administered only with the use of a computer, and includes auditory content. All other levels may be taken on a computer or in a paper-and-pencil format. Among levels, the exams differ in difficulty, length, and the types of questions which may appear. The Lower Level exam is shorter than the Middle or Upper level exams.

WHEN IS THE TEST ADMINISTERED?

Administration dates for the ISEE vary between test locations. ISEE test sites and administration dates can be found online, at ERBlearn.org. In addition to taking the test at a school that administers large group tests, students applying to grades 5-12 can register to take the ISEE at a Prometric Testing Center, which administers computer-based exams.

HOW MANY TIMES CAN I TAKE THE TEST?

Students may only take the ISEE once per admission season. The version of the test doesn't matter: a student who has taken a paper-and-pencil test may not take another test on a computer, and a student who has taken a computer-based test may not take another test in a paper-and-pencil format.

HOW DO I REGISTER?

The easiest and fastest way to register is to complete the **online application**. Visit www.ERBlearn.org to register for an exam in your area. It is also possible to register over the phone by calling (800) 446-0320 or (919) 956-8524, or to register by mail. To register by mail, you must complete and submit the application form available only in the printed ISEE student guide. Visit www.ERBlearn.org to order a printed copy of the ISEE student guide.

WHAT IS THE FORMAT OF THE ISEE?

The Lower, Middle, and Upper Level ISEE exams consist of four scored sections (**Verbal Reasoning**, **Quantitative Reasoning**, **Reading Comprehension**, and **Mathematics Achievement**), plus an **Essay** that is used as a writing sample. The format of the test differs based on the level of the exam:

LOWER LEVEL			
Section	**Questions**	**Length**	**Topics Covered**
Verbal Reasoning	34	20 min	Synonyms, Sentence Completion
Quantitative Reasoning	38	35 min	Logical Reasoning, Pattern Recognition (Word Problems)
Reading Comprehension	25	25 min	Short Passages
Math Achievement	30	30 min	Arithmetic, Algebra, Geometry, Data Analysis
Essay	1	30 min	One age-appropriate essay prompt
Total testing time: 2 hours 20 minutes			

MIDDLE AND UPPER LEVEL			
Section	**Questions**	**Length**	**Topics Covered**
Verbal Reasoning	40	20 min	Synonyms, Sentence Completion
Quantitative Reasoning	37	35 min	Logical Reasoning, Pattern Recognition (Word Problems and Quantitative Comparison)
Reading Comprehension	36	35 min	Short Passages
Math Achievement	47	40 min	Arithmetic, Algebra, Geometry, Data Analysis
Essay	1	30 min	One age-appropriate essay prompt
Total testing time: 2 hours 40 minutes			

Except for the Essay, all questions are **multiple-choice** (A) to (D). You are not normally allowed to use calculators, rulers, dictionaries, or other aids during the exam. However, students with documented learning disabilities or physical challenges may apply to take the test with extra time, aids, or other necessary accommodations that they receive in school. For more information about taking the ISEE with a documented disability, visit the ISEE Website at ERBlearn.org.

HOW IS THE ISEE SCORED?

All of the multiple-choice questions on the ISEE are equal in value, and your **raw score** for these sections is the total number of questions answered correctly. There is no penalty for incorrect answers.

Within each section, there are also 5-6 **experimental questions** that do not count towards your raw score for the section. The ISEE uses these questions to measure exam accuracy and to test material for upcoming exams. You won't be told which questions are the experimental questions, however, so you have to do your best on the entire section.

Your raw score for each section is then converted into a **scaled score** that represents how well you did in comparison to other students who have taken the same exam. Scaled scores range from about 760-950 for each section, with total scaled scores ranging from about 2280-2850.

The **Essay** is not scored, but is sent to the schools you are applying to as a sample of your writing skills. Admissions officers may use your essay to evaluate your writing ability when they are making admissions decisions.

Scores are released to families, and to the schools that families have designated as recipients, within 7-10 business days after the test date. Scores will be mailed to the address you provided when registering for the ISEE, and to up to six schools and/or counselors. You may request expedited score reports, or send score reports to additional schools or counselors, for an additional fee.

WHAT ARE THE ISEE PERCENTILES AND STANINES?

The ISEE score report also provides **ISEE percentile** rankings for each category, comparing your performance to that of other students in the same grade who have taken the test in the past three years. If you score in the 60th percentile, this means you are scoring higher than 60% of other students in your grade taking the exam.

These percentile rankings provide a more accurate way of evaluating student performance at each grade level. However, the ISEE percentiles are a comparison against only other students who have taken the ISEE, and these tend to be very high-achieving students. Students should not be discouraged if their percentile rankings appear low.

The following chart shows the median (50th percentile) ISEE scores for students applying to grades 5-12.

MEDIAN SCORES (ISEE 50TH PERCENTILE) FOR 2012					
Level	**Grade Applying To**	**Verbal Reasoning**	**Quantitative Reasoning**	**Reading Comprehension**	**Mathematics Achievement**
Lower Level	5	840	843	834	848
	6	856	856	848	863
Middle Level	7	863	865	866	871
	8	869	871	871	876
Upper Level	9	879	878	880	882
	10	883	882	886	886
	11	886	885	889	890
	12	881	884	880	889

The ISEE score report also includes **stanine** rankings. A stanine is a number from 1-9 obtained by dividing the entire range of students' scores into 9 segments, as shown in the table below:

percentile rank	stanine
1 – 3	1
4 – 10	2
11 – 22	3
23 – 39	4
40 – 59	5
60 – 76	6
77 – 88	7

89 – 95	8
96 – 99	9

Stanine scores are provided because small differences in percentile rankings may not represent a significant difference in ability. Stanines represent a range of percentile rankings, and are intended to provide a better representation of student ability.

HOW DO SCHOOLS USE THE ISEE?

Schools use the ISEE as one way to assess potential applicants, but it is by no means the only tool that they are using. Schools also pay very close attention to the rest of a student's application—academic record, teacher recommendations, extracurricular activities, writing samples, and interviews—in order to determine which students might be the best fit for their program. The personal components of a student's application sometimes give schools a lot more information about the student's personality and potential contributions to the school's overall community. Different schools place a different amount of importance on ISEE and other test scores within this process, and admissions offices are good places to find out how much your schools of interest will weight the ISEE.

TEST-TAKING STRATEGIES

CHAPTER 2

APPROACHING THE ISEE

SECTION 1

Before you review the content covered on the ISEE, you need to focus on *how* you take the ISEE. If you approach the ISEE *thoughtfully* and *strategically*, you will avoid common traps and tricks planted in the ISEE by the test makers. Think of the ISEE as a timed maze—you need to make every turn cleverly and quickly so that you avoid getting stuck at a dead end with no time to spare.

In this section, you will learn about the ISEE's format and structure; this awareness will help you avoid any surprises or shocks on test day. The ISEE is a very predictable exam and will seem less challenging once you understand what it looks like and how it works. By learning and practicing the best test-taking strategies and techniques, you will discover how to work as quickly and efficiently as possible. Once you know what to expect, you can refine your knowledge of the actual material tested on the ISEE, such as the verbal and math skills that are based on your grade level in school.

This section on ISEE strategies will answer the following **major questions**:

1. How does the ISEE differ from a test you take in school?
2. What preparation strategies can you learn before you take the ISEE?
3. What strategies can you learn to use during the ISEE?
4. How can you manage stress before and during the ISEE?

In the process of answering your big questions, this section will also highlight key facts about smart test-taking:

- Your answer choice matters—your process does not. Enter your answer choices correctly and carefully to earn points. You have a set amount of time per section, so spend it wisely.
- The ISEE's format and directions do not change, so learn them now.
- All questions have the same value.
- Each level of the ISEE corresponds to a range of grades, and score expectations differ based on your grade level.
- Identify your areas of strength and weakness, and review any content that feels unfamiliar.

- Apply universal strategies—prediction-making, Process of Elimination, back-solving, and educated guessing—to the multiple-choice sections.
- Stay calm and be confident in your abilities as you prepare for and take the ISEE.

HOW DOES THE ISEE DIFFER FROM A TEST YOU TAKE IN SCHOOL?

The ISEE differs from tests you take in school in four major ways:

1. It is not concerned with the process behind your answers. Your answer is either right or wrong: there is no partial credit.
2. You have a set amount of time per section (and for the exam as a whole).
3. It is divided into four levels that correspond to four grade ranges of students.
4. It is extremely predictable given that its format, structure, and directions never vary.

NO PARTIAL CREDIT

At this point in your school career, you have probably heard your teacher remark, "Be sure to show your work on the test!" You are most likely familiar with almost every teacher's policy of "No work, no credit." However, the ISEE completely ignores this guideline. The machine that grades your exam does not care that you penciled brilliant logic in the margins of the test booklet—the machine only looks at your answer choice. Your answer choice is either right or wrong: **there is no partial credit**.

SET AMOUNT OF TIME

You have a **set amount of time per section**, so spend it wisely. The ISEE test proctors will never award you extra time after a test section has ended because you spent half of one section struggling valiantly on a single problem. Instead, you must learn to work within each section's time constraints.

You also must view the questions as equal because **each question is worth the same number of points** (one). Even though some questions are more challenging than others, they all carry the same weight. Rather than dwell on a problem, you should skip it, work through the rest of the section, and come back to it if you have time.

FOUR LEVELS

There are four levels of the ISEE—Primary, Lower, Middle, and Upper—each of which is administered to a specific range of students. The Primary Level is given to students applying to grades 2, 3, and 4; the Lower Level is given to students applying to grades 5 and 6; the Middle Level is given to students applying to grades 7 and 8; and the Upper Level is given to students applying to grades 9, 10, 11, and 12. While you might be used to taking tests in school that are completely tailored to your grade, the ISEE is different: each test level covers content for a specific range of grade levels.

Score expectations differ based on your grade level. You are not expected to answer every question correctly on an Upper Level exam if you are only in eighth grade. Conversely, if you are in eleventh grade, you are expected to answer the most questions correctly on the Upper Level exam because you are one of the oldest students taking that exam.

STANDARD FORMAT

The ISEE is, by definition, a **standardized test**, which means that its format and directions are standard and predictable. While your teachers might change formats and directions for every assessment they administer, you can expect to see the same format and directions on every ISEE.

WHAT PREPARATION STRATEGIES CAN YOU LEARN BEFORE YOU TAKE THE ISEE?

Now that you are familiar with how the ISEE differs from the tests you take in school, you are ready to learn some test tips. You can prepare for the ISEE by following these three steps:

1. Learn the format and directions of the test.
2. Identify your areas of strength and weakness.
3. Create a study schedule to review and practice test content.

LEARN THE FORMAT AND DIRECTIONS

The structure of the ISEE is entirely predictable, so learn this now. Rather than wasting precious time reading the directions and understanding the format on test day, take the time now to familiarize yourself with the test's format and directions.

Refer to the tables on pages 6 and 7 for an overview of the ISEE's format. Continue reading for specific directions for the Verbal Reasoning, Reading Comprehension, and Essay sections. Specific directions for the Quantitative Reasoning and Mathematics Achievement sections can be found in Ivy Global's *ISEE Math*.

IDENTIFY YOUR STRENGTHS AND WEAKNESSES

To determine your areas of strength and weakness and to get an idea of which concepts you need to review, take a full-length, accurate practice exam to serve as a diagnostic test. Practice exams for the ISEE can be found in this book.

Make sure you simulate test day conditions by timing yourself. Then, check your answers against the correct answers. Write down how many questions you missed in each section, and note the topics or types of questions you found most challenging. What was hard about the test? What did you feel good about? Did you leave a lot of questions blank because of timing issues, or did you leave questions blank because you did not know how to solve them? Reflecting on these questions, in addition to looking at your score breakdown, will help you determine your strengths, weaknesses, and areas for improvement.

CREATE A STUDY SCHEDULE

After determining your areas of strength and weakness, create a study plan and schedule for your ISEE preparation to review content. Work backward from your test date until you arrive at your starting point for studying. The number of weeks you have until your exam will determine how much time you can (and should) devote to your preparation. Remember, practice is the most important thing!

To begin, try using this sample study plan as a model for your own personalized study schedule.

SAMPLE STUDY PLAN

My test date is: _________________.

I have ____ weeks to study. I will make an effort to study ____ minutes/hours each night, and I will set aside extra time on ________________ to take timed sections.

I plan to take ____ full-length tests between now and my test date. I will study for ____ weeks and then take a practice test. My goal for this test is to improve my score in the following sections:

____

____

____

____

____

____

____

____

If I do not make this goal, then I will spend more time studying.

STUDY SCHEDULE				
Date	**Plan of Study**	**Time Allotted**	**Time Spent**	**Goal Reached?**
1/1	Learn 5 words and review perimeter of polygons	1 hour	44 minutes	Yes, I know 5 new words and can calculate perimeter!
1/3	Learn 5 words and review area of triangles	1 hour	1 hour	I know 5 new words, but I'm still confused about the area of triangles. I'll review this again next time and ask a teacher, tutor, or parent for help.

WHAT STRATEGIES CAN YOU LEARN TO USE DURING THE TEST?

Once you have grown accustomed to the ISEE through practice, you are ready to learn strategies to use during the ISEE. The following points will prepare you to take the test as cleverly and efficiently as possible:

1. Enter your answer choices correctly and carefully.
2. Pace yourself to manage your time effectively.
3. Learn a strategic approach for multiple-choice questions.

ENTERING ANSWER CHOICES

Whether you are taking a pencil-and-paper or a computer-based exam, you must follow the directions carefully to enter your answers. In school you probably take tests that, for the most part, do not ask you to enter your answers in a specific format. However, the ISEE streamlines the grading process by only reviewing the answers you have entered on your answer sheet or into the computer program. This means that any notes or work you have written on your scratch paper will not be reviewed, and you will only receive credit for entering your answers correctly.

On a computer-based exam, you will click an answer on the computer screen in order to enter your response. Follow the directions carefully to make sure your answer has been recorded. Within each section, you will be able to go back to questions earlier in the section and change your answers. You will also be able to skip questions and come back to them later. However, you will not be able to review questions from sections that come earlier or later in the exam; you will only be able to review your answers for the questions in the section you are currently working on. Make sure all of your answers have been entered correctly before your time is up for the section.

On a pencil-and-paper exam, you will enter your answers on a separate answer sheet. You must grid in your multiple-choice answers onto this sheet using an HB pencil to fill in the circle that corresponds to your answer. This sheet is scanned and scored by a highly sensitive computer. You will also write your Essay on separate lined pages of this answer sheet.

Since you have to take an additional step to record your answers, it is important that you avoid making gridding mistakes. Sadly, many students get confused and mismark their answer sheets. Remember, even if you arrive at the right answer, it is only correct and counted in your favor if you grid correctly on your answer sheet.

To grid correctly and carefully to maximize your points, consider the following tips:

Keep your answer sheet neat. Since your answer sheet is graded by a machine, your score is calculated based on what your marks look like. The machine cannot know what you really meant if you picked the wrong bubble. Stray marks can harm your score, especially if you darken the correct answer but accidentally make a mark that confuses the machine! Avoid this and other errors by consulting the following image, which shows the difference between answers that are properly shaded and those that are not.

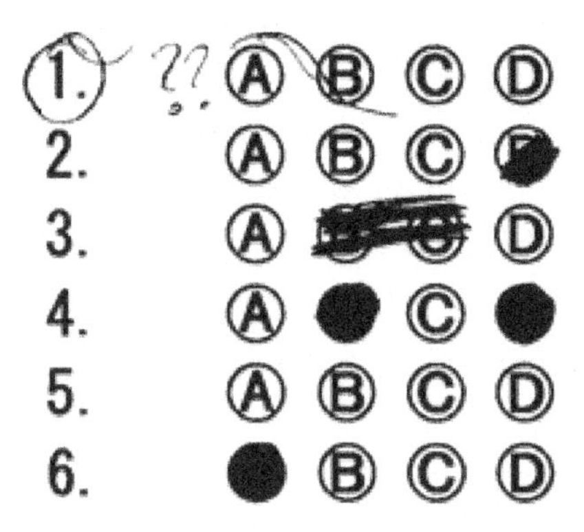

Answer 1 is *wrong* because no answer is selected and there are stray marks.
Answer 2 is *wrong* because choice (D) has not been darkened completely.
Answer 3 is *wrong* because two answers have been partially selected.
Answer 4 is *wrong* because two answers have been selected.
Answer 5 is *neither right nor wrong* because it was left blank.
Answer 6 is *right* because choice (A) has been darkened properly.

Train yourself to **circle your answer choice in your test booklet**. If you have time to go back and check your answers, you can easily check your circled answers against your gridded ones.

You should also **create a system for marking questions that you skipped** or that you found confusing (see the next section for more information about skipping questions). Try circling those question numbers only in your test booklet so that you can find them later if you want to solve them or check your work. Be aware of these questions when gridding answers on your answer sheet.

Finally, **grid your answers in batches of four, five, or six answer choices.** That way, you do not have to go back and forth between your test booklet and your answer sheet every minute. If you choose to use this strategy, keep an eye on the clock—you do not want to get to the end of the section and find you have not gridded any answers. Depending on how much time you have left to check your work (if you happen to finish early), you can either review every problem or spot-check a series of questions on your answer sheet against your test booklet.

TIME MANAGEMENT (PACING)

Manage your time effectively to boost your score. The ISEE has an element of time pressure, so it is important to keep moving on the exam rather than spending too much time on any single question.

You can come back to questions within each section of the ISEE. Each question is only worth one point, regardless of its difficulty. If you are stuck on a problem, you should make your best guess and move on to try to answer another problem. It makes more sense to answer as many questions as possible (and get as many points as possible) rather than spending all your time on one question. If you come across a question you want to come back to, circle it in your question booklet or mark it on your scratch paper. Remember not to make any stray marks on your answer sheet.

By moving quickly through each question of the section, you will ensure that: 1) you see every question in the section; 2) you gain points on questions that are easy for you; 3) you return to more challenging problems and figure out as many as you can with your remaining time. It is also important to note that you might not be able to answer several questions in each section if you are on the younger end of the testing group for your particular test level. In that case, you should make your best guess based on the information you do know, but shouldn't worry if the content is unfamiliar.

Even if you are unsure about a question and want to come back to it later, you should **always make a guess.** The ISEE doesn't take off any points for answering questions incorrectly, so you should never leave a question blank! Even if you guess a completely random answer, you have a small chance of gaining a point. If you can rule out one or two choices that you know are wrong, you have even better odds of guessing the right answer. Therefore, always make a guess on every question, even if you are planning to come back to it later. When your time is up, you want to make sure that you have entered an answer for every question!

Follow this step-by-step process for moving through a section:

1. Look through the section and answer the questions that are easy for you. If a question seems difficult or is taking too long, make a guess and circle it to come back to later.
2. After answering all the easier questions, go back to the questions you have circled and spend some time working on ones that you think you might be able to solve. If you figure out that the answer you originally guessed was incorrect, change that answer on your answer sheet.
3. If you have no idea how to solve a question, leave your best guess as your answer.
4. If you have any time remaining, check your work for the questions you solved.

STRATEGIES FOR MULTIPLE-CHOICE QUESTIONS

Apply universal strategies—prediction-making, Process of Elimination, back-solving, and educated guessing—to the multiple-choice sections. To illustrate the value of these strategies, read through the following example of a synonym question from the Verbal Reasoning section:

HAPPY:

(A) delighted
(B) unhappy
(C) crazy
(D) nice

Answer: (A). "Delighted" is the correct answer because it is the word that most nearly means "happy."

Regardless of whether the answer choices are easy, difficult, or somewhere in between, you can use certain tricks and tips to your advantage. To approach ISEE questions effectively, you need to step into the test makers' minds and learn to avoid their traps.

Make predictions. When you see a question, try to come up with an answer on your own before looking at the answer choices. You can literally cover the answer choices with your hand so that you must rely on your own intelligence to predict an answer instead of being swayed by answer choices that you see. If you look at the answer choices first, you might be tempted to pick an answer without thinking about the other options and what the question is asking you. Instead, make a prediction so that you understand the question fully and get a clear sense of what to look for in the answers. In the synonym example above, you could predict that a possible synonym for "happy" would be something like "glad."

Use the Process of Elimination. For each multiple-choice question, you must realize that the answer is right in front of you. To narrow down your answer choices, think about the potential incorrect answers and actively identify those to eliminate them. Even if you can eliminate just one answer, you will set yourself up for better odds if you decide to guess. For the synonym example above, test your prediction of "glad" against the answer choices and immediately eliminate "unhappy" since it is opposite in meaning. You can also probably eliminate "crazy" and "nice" since those words do not match your prediction. This leaves you with "delighted," which is the correct answer.

Try back-solving. This strategy is most useful on the math sections, especially when you are given a complicated, multi-step word problem. Instead of writing an equation, try plugging in the answer choices to the word problem. Take a look at the following question:

Catherine has a basket of candy. On Monday, she eats ½ of all the candy. On Tuesday, she eats 2 pieces. On Wednesday, she eats twice the amount of candy that she consumed on Tuesday. If she only has 4 pieces left on Thursday, how many pieces did she initially have?

(A) 12

(B) 14

(C) 16

(D) 20

To use back-solving, start with answer choice (C) and plug it into the word problem. If (C) is the correct answer, you are done. If not, you will then know whether you should test (B) or (D). When we start with 16 pieces of candy, we subtract 8 on Monday, then 2 more for Tuesday, and then 4 more for Wednesday. By Thursday, Catherine only has two pieces of candy left, which is less than the amount we wanted. Therefore, we know our answer has to be bigger, so we eliminate choices (A), (B), and (C) and try (D), which works.

(*Fun Fact:* If you think about it, you will have to plug in three answer choices at most to determine the right answer.)

Armed with these strategies, you might feel that the ISEE is starting to look more manageable because you now have shortcuts that will help you navigate the maze of questions quickly and cleverly.

Take a look at this example to practice using the strategies you just read about.

Because Kaitlin was -------- from her soccer game, she went to bed early.

(A) thrilled

(B) exhausted

(C) competitive

(D) inspired

1. Assess the question and recognize what it is testing. In this case, the question tests whether you can pick a word to complete the sentence.
2. Make a prediction. What about Kaitlin's soccer game would cause her to go to bed early? Maybe it wore her out, so we could look for something like "tired" to go in the blank.
3. Look for inaccurate answer choices and eliminate them. If Kaitlin were "thrilled," "competitive," or "inspired" as a result of her soccer game, this wouldn't explain why she had to go to bed early. Therefore, you can eliminate answers (A), (C), and (D).

4. Make an educated guess, or choose the answer you feel most confident about. Since you made a fantastic prediction and used Process of Elimination, you only have one choice left: (B). "Exhausted" is the correct answer—you just earned yourself a point!

HOW CAN YOU MANAGE YOUR STRESS?

If you have ever taken a big test before, or had an important sports match, play, or presentation, then you know what anxiety feels like. Even if you are excited for an approaching event, you might feel nervous. You might begin to doubt yourself, and you might feel as if your mind is racing while butterflies flutter in your stomach!

When it comes to preparing for the ISEE, the good news is that a little anxiety (or adrenaline) goes a long way. Anxiety is a natural, motivating force that will help you study hard in the days leading up to your test. That anxiety will also help you stay alert and work efficiently during the test.

Sometimes, however, anxiety might become larger than life and start to get the best of you. To prevent anxiety and nerves from clouding your ability to work effectively and believe in yourself, you should try some of the suggestions below. Many of these suggestions are good ideas to use in everyday life, but they become especially important in the final week before your test and on test day itself.

- **Relax and slow down.** To center yourself and ease your anxiety, take a big, deep breath. Slowly inhale for a few seconds and then slowly exhale for a few seconds. Shut your eyes and relax. Stretch your arms, roll your neck gently, crack your knuckles—get in the zone of Zen! Continue to breathe deeply and slowly until you can literally feel your body calm down.
- **Picture your goals.** Close your eyes or just pause to reflect on what you want to achieve on test day. Visualize your success, whether that means simply answering all the math questions or getting a top score and gaining acceptance into the school of your dreams. Acknowledge your former successes and abilities, and believe in yourself.
- **Break it down.** Instead of trying to study a whole section at once, break up your studying into small and manageable chunks. Outline your study goals before you start. For example, instead of trying to master the entire Reading Comprehension section at once, you might want to work on one type of passage at a time.
- **Sleep.** Make sure you get plenty of rest and sleep, especially the two nights leading up to your exam!
- **Fuel up.** Eat healthy, filling meals that fuel your brain. Also, drink lots of water to stay hydrated.
- **Take a break.** Put down the books and go play outside, read, listen to music, exercise, or have a good conversation with friend or family member. A good break can be just as restful as a nap. However, watching television will provide minimal relaxation.

On the night before the exam, study only lightly. Make a list of your three biggest fears and work on them, but don't try to learn anything new. Pick out what you are going to wear to the exam—try wearing layers in case the exam room is hotter or colder than you expect. Organize everything you need to bring. Know where the test center is located and how long it will take to get there. Have a nutritious meal and get plenty of sleep!

On the morning of the exam, let your adrenaline kick in naturally. Eat a good breakfast and stay hydrated; your body needs fuel to endure the test. Bring along several pencils and a good eraser. Listen carefully to the test proctor's instructions and let the proctor know if you are left-handed so you can sit at an appropriate desk. Take a deep breath and remember: you are smart and accomplished! Believe in yourself and you will do just fine.

PRACTICE TESTS

CHAPTER 3

PRACTICE TEST 1

UPPER LEVEL

HOW TO TAKE THIS PRACTICE TEST

To simulate an accurate testing environment, sit at a desk in a quiet location free of distractions—no TV, computers, phones, music, or noise—and clear your desk of all materials except pencils and erasers. Remember that no calculators, rulers, protractors, dictionaries, or other aids are allowed on the ISEE.

Give yourself the following amounts of time for each section:

SECTION	SUBJECT	TIME LIMIT
1	Verbal Reasoning	20 minutes
2	Quantitative Reasoning	35 minutes
5 minute break		
3	Reading Comprehension	25 minutes
4	Mathematics Achievement	30 minutes
5 minute break		
5	Essay	30 minutes

Have an adult help you monitor your time, or use a watch and time yourself. Only give yourself the allotted time for each section; put your pencil down when your time is up.

Follow the instructions carefully. As you take your test, bubble your answers into the answer sheets provided. Use the test booklet as scratch paper for notes and calculations. Remember that you are not granted time at the end of a section to transfer your answers to the answer sheet, so you must do this as you go along.

When you are finished, check your answers against the answer keys provided. Then, score your exam using the directions at the end of the book.

Note: students with diagnosed learning disabilities who apply for testing with accommodations may receive extra time, or may be allowed to use certain assistive devices during the ISEE. For more information, visit http://erblearn.org/parents/admission/isee/accommodations.

Ivy Global

ISEE
UPPER LEVEL TEST 1

MARKING INSTRUCTIONS

- Use a #2 or HB pencil only on pages 34 and 35.
- Use a ballpoint pen for your essay on pages 36 and 37.
- Make dark marks that completely fill the circle.
- Erase clearly any mark you wish to change.
- Make no stray marks on this form.
- Do not fold or crease this form.

Correct Mark

Incorrect Marks

1 VERBAL REASONING

1	Ⓐ Ⓑ Ⓒ Ⓓ	15	Ⓐ Ⓑ Ⓒ Ⓓ	29	Ⓐ Ⓑ Ⓒ Ⓓ
2	Ⓐ Ⓑ Ⓒ Ⓓ	16	Ⓐ Ⓑ Ⓒ Ⓓ	30	Ⓐ Ⓑ Ⓒ Ⓓ
3	Ⓐ Ⓑ Ⓒ Ⓓ	17	Ⓐ Ⓑ Ⓒ Ⓓ	31	Ⓐ Ⓑ Ⓒ Ⓓ
4	Ⓐ Ⓑ Ⓒ Ⓓ	18	Ⓐ Ⓑ Ⓒ Ⓓ	32	Ⓐ Ⓑ Ⓒ Ⓓ
5	Ⓐ Ⓑ Ⓒ Ⓓ	19	Ⓐ Ⓑ Ⓒ Ⓓ	33	Ⓐ Ⓑ Ⓒ Ⓓ
6	Ⓐ Ⓑ Ⓒ Ⓓ	20	Ⓐ Ⓑ Ⓒ Ⓓ	34	Ⓐ Ⓑ Ⓒ Ⓓ Lower Level Ends
7	Ⓐ Ⓑ Ⓒ Ⓓ	21	Ⓐ Ⓑ Ⓒ Ⓓ	35	Ⓐ Ⓑ Ⓒ Ⓓ
8	Ⓐ Ⓑ Ⓒ Ⓓ	22	Ⓐ Ⓑ Ⓒ Ⓓ	36	Ⓐ Ⓑ Ⓒ Ⓓ
9	Ⓐ Ⓑ Ⓒ Ⓓ	23	Ⓐ Ⓑ Ⓒ Ⓓ	37	Ⓐ Ⓑ Ⓒ Ⓓ
10	Ⓐ Ⓑ Ⓒ Ⓓ	24	Ⓐ Ⓑ Ⓒ Ⓓ	38	Ⓐ Ⓑ Ⓒ Ⓓ
11	Ⓐ Ⓑ Ⓒ Ⓓ	25	Ⓐ Ⓑ Ⓒ Ⓓ	39	Ⓐ Ⓑ Ⓒ Ⓓ
12	Ⓐ Ⓑ Ⓒ Ⓓ	26	Ⓐ Ⓑ Ⓒ Ⓓ	40	Ⓐ Ⓑ Ⓒ Ⓓ Middle/Upper Level Ends
13	Ⓐ Ⓑ Ⓒ Ⓓ	27	Ⓐ Ⓑ Ⓒ Ⓓ		
14	Ⓐ Ⓑ Ⓒ Ⓓ	28	Ⓐ Ⓑ Ⓒ Ⓓ		

2 QUANTITATIVE REASONING

1 Ⓐ Ⓑ Ⓒ Ⓓ	15 Ⓐ Ⓑ Ⓒ Ⓓ	29 Ⓐ Ⓑ Ⓒ Ⓓ
2 Ⓐ Ⓑ Ⓒ Ⓓ	16 Ⓐ Ⓑ Ⓒ Ⓓ	30 Ⓐ Ⓑ Ⓒ Ⓓ
3 Ⓐ Ⓑ Ⓒ Ⓓ	17 Ⓐ Ⓑ Ⓒ Ⓓ	31 Ⓐ Ⓑ Ⓒ Ⓓ
4 Ⓐ Ⓑ Ⓒ Ⓓ	18 Ⓐ Ⓑ Ⓒ Ⓓ	32 Ⓐ Ⓑ Ⓒ Ⓓ
5 Ⓐ Ⓑ Ⓒ Ⓓ	19 Ⓐ Ⓑ Ⓒ Ⓓ	33 Ⓐ Ⓑ Ⓒ Ⓓ
6 Ⓐ Ⓑ Ⓒ Ⓓ	20 Ⓐ Ⓑ Ⓒ Ⓓ	34 Ⓐ Ⓑ Ⓒ Ⓓ
7 Ⓐ Ⓑ Ⓒ Ⓓ	21 Ⓐ Ⓑ Ⓒ Ⓓ	35 Ⓐ Ⓑ Ⓒ Ⓓ
8 Ⓐ Ⓑ Ⓒ Ⓓ	22 Ⓐ Ⓑ Ⓒ Ⓓ	36 Ⓐ Ⓑ Ⓒ Ⓓ
9 Ⓐ Ⓑ Ⓒ Ⓓ	23 Ⓐ Ⓑ Ⓒ Ⓓ	37 Ⓐ Ⓑ Ⓒ Ⓓ **Middle/Upper Level Ends**
10 Ⓐ Ⓑ Ⓒ Ⓓ	24 Ⓐ Ⓑ Ⓒ Ⓓ	38 Ⓐ Ⓑ Ⓒ Ⓓ **Lower Level Ends**
11 Ⓐ Ⓑ Ⓒ Ⓓ	25 Ⓐ Ⓑ Ⓒ Ⓓ	
12 Ⓐ Ⓑ Ⓒ Ⓓ	26 Ⓐ Ⓑ Ⓒ Ⓓ	
13 Ⓐ Ⓑ Ⓒ Ⓓ	27 Ⓐ Ⓑ Ⓒ Ⓓ	
14 Ⓐ Ⓑ Ⓒ Ⓓ	28 Ⓐ Ⓑ Ⓒ Ⓓ	

3 READING COMPREHENSION

1 Ⓐ Ⓑ Ⓒ Ⓓ	15 Ⓐ Ⓑ Ⓒ Ⓓ	29 Ⓐ Ⓑ Ⓒ Ⓓ
2 Ⓐ Ⓑ Ⓒ Ⓓ	16 Ⓐ Ⓑ Ⓒ Ⓓ	30 Ⓐ Ⓑ Ⓒ Ⓓ
3 Ⓐ Ⓑ Ⓒ Ⓓ	17 Ⓐ Ⓑ Ⓒ Ⓓ	31 Ⓐ Ⓑ Ⓒ Ⓓ
4 Ⓐ Ⓑ Ⓒ Ⓓ	18 Ⓐ Ⓑ Ⓒ Ⓓ	32 Ⓐ Ⓑ Ⓒ Ⓓ
5 Ⓐ Ⓑ Ⓒ Ⓓ	19 Ⓐ Ⓑ Ⓒ Ⓓ	33 Ⓐ Ⓑ Ⓒ Ⓓ
6 Ⓐ Ⓑ Ⓒ Ⓓ	20 Ⓐ Ⓑ Ⓒ Ⓓ	34 Ⓐ Ⓑ Ⓒ Ⓓ
7 Ⓐ Ⓑ Ⓒ Ⓓ	21 Ⓐ Ⓑ Ⓒ Ⓓ	35 Ⓐ Ⓑ Ⓒ Ⓓ
8 Ⓐ Ⓑ Ⓒ Ⓓ	22 Ⓐ Ⓑ Ⓒ Ⓓ	36 Ⓐ Ⓑ Ⓒ Ⓓ **Middle/Upper Level Ends**
9 Ⓐ Ⓑ Ⓒ Ⓓ	23 Ⓐ Ⓑ Ⓒ Ⓓ	
10 Ⓐ Ⓑ Ⓒ Ⓓ	24 Ⓐ Ⓑ Ⓒ Ⓓ	
11 Ⓐ Ⓑ Ⓒ Ⓓ	25 Ⓐ Ⓑ Ⓒ Ⓓ **Lower Level Ends**	
12 Ⓐ Ⓑ Ⓒ Ⓓ	26 Ⓐ Ⓑ Ⓒ Ⓓ	
13 Ⓐ Ⓑ Ⓒ Ⓓ	27 Ⓐ Ⓑ Ⓒ Ⓓ	
14 Ⓐ Ⓑ Ⓒ Ⓓ	28 Ⓐ Ⓑ Ⓒ Ⓓ	

4 MATHEMATICS ACHIEVEMENT

1 Ⓐ Ⓑ Ⓒ Ⓓ	18 Ⓐ Ⓑ Ⓒ Ⓓ	35 Ⓐ Ⓑ Ⓒ Ⓓ
2 Ⓐ Ⓑ Ⓒ Ⓓ	19 Ⓐ Ⓑ Ⓒ Ⓓ	36 Ⓐ Ⓑ Ⓒ Ⓓ
3 Ⓐ Ⓑ Ⓒ Ⓓ	20 Ⓐ Ⓑ Ⓒ Ⓓ	37 Ⓐ Ⓑ Ⓒ Ⓓ
4 Ⓐ Ⓑ Ⓒ Ⓓ	21 Ⓐ Ⓑ Ⓒ Ⓓ	38 Ⓐ Ⓑ Ⓒ Ⓓ
5 Ⓐ Ⓑ Ⓒ Ⓓ	22 Ⓐ Ⓑ Ⓒ Ⓓ	39 Ⓐ Ⓑ Ⓒ Ⓓ
6 Ⓐ Ⓑ Ⓒ Ⓓ	23 Ⓐ Ⓑ Ⓒ Ⓓ	40 Ⓐ Ⓑ Ⓒ Ⓓ
7 Ⓐ Ⓑ Ⓒ Ⓓ	24 Ⓐ Ⓑ Ⓒ Ⓓ	41 Ⓐ Ⓑ Ⓒ Ⓓ
8 Ⓐ Ⓑ Ⓒ Ⓓ	25 Ⓐ Ⓑ Ⓒ Ⓓ	42 Ⓐ Ⓑ Ⓒ Ⓓ
9 Ⓐ Ⓑ Ⓒ Ⓓ	26 Ⓐ Ⓑ Ⓒ Ⓓ	43 Ⓐ Ⓑ Ⓒ Ⓓ
10 Ⓐ Ⓑ Ⓒ Ⓓ	27 Ⓐ Ⓑ Ⓒ Ⓓ	44 Ⓐ Ⓑ Ⓒ Ⓓ
11 Ⓐ Ⓑ Ⓒ Ⓓ	28 Ⓐ Ⓑ Ⓒ Ⓓ	45 Ⓐ Ⓑ Ⓒ Ⓓ
12 Ⓐ Ⓑ Ⓒ Ⓓ	29 Ⓐ Ⓑ Ⓒ Ⓓ	46 Ⓐ Ⓑ Ⓒ Ⓓ
13 Ⓐ Ⓑ Ⓒ Ⓓ	30 Ⓐ Ⓑ Ⓒ Ⓓ **Lower Level Ends**	47 Ⓐ Ⓑ Ⓒ Ⓓ **Middle/Upper Level Ends**
14 Ⓐ Ⓑ Ⓒ Ⓓ	31 Ⓐ Ⓑ Ⓒ Ⓓ	
15 Ⓐ Ⓑ Ⓒ Ⓓ	32 Ⓐ Ⓑ Ⓒ Ⓓ	
16 Ⓐ Ⓑ Ⓒ Ⓓ	33 Ⓐ Ⓑ Ⓒ Ⓓ	
17 Ⓐ Ⓑ Ⓒ Ⓓ	34 Ⓐ Ⓑ Ⓒ Ⓓ	

STUDENT NAME ______________________ GRADE APPLYING FOR __________

Use a blue or black ballpoint pen to write the final draft of your essay on this sheet.

You must write your essay topic in this space.

Use specific details and examples in your response.

Section 1
Verbal Reasoning

40 Questions | **Time: 20 minutes**

This section is divided into two parts that contain two different types of questions. As soon as you have completed Part One, answer the questions in Part Two. You may write in your test booklet. For each answer you select, fill in the corresponding circle on your answer document.

PART ONE — SYNONYMS

Each question in Part One consists of a word in capital letters followed by four answer choices. Select the one word that is most nearly the same in meaning as the word in capital letters.

SAMPLE QUESTION:

CHARGE:

(A) release
(B) belittle
(C) accuse
(D) conspire

Sample Answer

Ⓐ Ⓑ ● Ⓓ

The correct answer is "accuse," so circle C is darkened.

Go on to the next page ➡

PART TWO — SENTENCE COMPLETION

Each question in Part Two is made up of a sentence with one blank. Each blank indicates that a word or phrase is missing. The sentence is followed by four answer choices. Select the word or phrase that will best complete the meaning of the sentence as a whole.

SAMPLE QUESTIONS: | Sample Answer

It rained so much that the streets were -------. ● Ⓑ Ⓒ Ⓓ

(A) flooded
(B) arid
(C) paved
(D) crowded

The correct answer is "flooded," so circle A is darkened.

The house was so dirty that it took -------. Ⓐ Ⓑ Ⓒ ●

(A) less than ten minutes to wash it.
(B) four months to demolish it.
(C) over a week to walk across it.
(D) two days to clean it.

The correct answer is "two days to clean it," so circle D is darkened.

STOP. Do not go on until told to do so.

PART ONE – SYNONYMS

Directions: Select the word that is most nearly the same in meaning as the word in capital letters.

1. VANITY
   (A) conceit
   (B) greed
   (C) ruthlessness
   (D) imagination

2. IMMACULATE
   (A) shackled
   (B) warranted
   (C) indigo
   (D) flawless

3. TURBULENT
   (A) stormy
   (B) breathless
   (C) jumbled
   (D) obnoxious

4. LADEN
   (A) upheld
   (B) submerged
   (C) burdened
   (D) broken

5. EXPEDITE
   (A) construct
   (B) hurry
   (C) incite
   (D) record

6. ETERNAL
   (A) ephemeral
   (B) internal
   (C) final
   (D) infinite

7. BOLSTER
   (A) demolish
   (B) invite
   (C) support
   (D) lock

8. APPLICABLE
   (A) submissive
   (B) appropriate
   (C) open
   (D) apprehensive

9. EXPEDITIOUS
   (A) quick
   (B) jumpy
   (C) nervous
   (D) prior

10. DIPLOMAT
    (A) governor
    (B) ambassador
    (C) ally
    (D) friend

11. PLUMMET
    (A) indicate
    (B) celebrate
    (C) fall
    (D) hasten

12. FRAUD
    (A) deterrent
    (B) propaganda
    (C) coercion
    (D) deception

Go on to the next page ➡

13. DEDUCE
    (A) lessen
    (B) tutor
    (C) infer
    (D) demote

14. SWINDLE
    (A) open
    (B) invent
    (C) impoverish
    (D) cheat

15. INVISIBLE
    (A) silent
    (B) unseen
    (C) secure
    (D) unpredictable

16. JEER
    (A) mock
    (B) praise
    (C) annoy
    (D) activate

17. FRIVOLOUS
    (A) enjoyable
    (B) silly
    (C) outrageous
    (D) unseemly

18. EVADE
    (A) depart
    (B) defend
    (C) dislike
    (D) escape

19. SPRUCE
    (A) cleanliness
    (B) evergreen
    (C) broom
    (D) virtue

Go on to the next page ➡

PART TWO – SENTENCE COMPLETION

Directions: Select the word that best completes the sentence.

20. While many actors are melodramatic in their portrayals of characters, Morgan Freeman is known for his more -------- acting technique.
    (A) noisy
    (B) enthusiastic
    (C) subtle
    (D) excruciating

21. The sloth received its name for its -------- movements; it can take an hour for it to move a few feet.
    (A) shaky
    (B) rapid
    (C) vicious
    (D) languid

22. The mechanic's repairs were only ---------; the car looked much better, but the engine still wouldn't start.
    (A) ingenious
    (B) unoriginal
    (C) superficial
    (D) simplistic

23. Mules have a reputation for -------- behavior, but they're actually quite compliant when treated properly.
    (A) jubilant
    (B) bored
    (C) focused
    (D) obstinate

24. The beginning of the flu is usually marked by --------; patients are tired and unable to get out of bed.
    (A) fervor
    (B) fatigue
    (C) dread
    (D) amusement

25. Although Bob was very --------, he still lacked the practical knowledge to take proper care of himself.
    (A) childish
    (B) sublime
    (C) pragmatic
    (D) intelligent

26. Because our debate club picks very -------- topics, we often have heated debates.
    (A) unknown
    (B) contentious
    (C) delightful
    (D) lighthearted

27. James Crawford's famous song "Jock-a-mo" had an -------- beat, which induced listeners to clap and move along with the music.
    (A) airy
    (B) intangible
    (C) uncouth
    (D) infectious

Go on to the next page ➜

28. Since she is usually interested in studying chemistry, Christine's -------- attitude toward the chemistry professor's presentation was surprising.

    (A) inane
    (B) engaged
    (C) apathetic
    (D) graceful

29. The -------- play of accident-prone children often stands in sharp contrast to the vigilance of their careful parents.

    (A) quiet
    (B) heedless
    (C) uninterrupted
    (D) obnoxious

30. When trekking through the desert, it is important to carry some form of liquid to -------- one's inevitable thirst.

    (A) foster
    (B) kick
    (C) brew
    (D) quench

31. The Salem witch trials led to the unfair -------- of many innocent people whose only indictments were the words of confused or dishonest witnesses.

    (A) persecution
    (B) release
    (C) competition
    (D) transformation

32. Though many people find Brussels sprouts quite a -------- vegetable, others find them -------- and refuse to eat them.

    (A) savory...average
    (B) horrendous...annoying
    (C) tasty...repugnant
    (D) starchy...arcane

33. In some circles, George Orwell has been -------- as a prophet for -------- the real-world rise of mass surveillance in his dark, fictional novel, *1984*.

    (A) derided...preventing
    (B) promoted...endorsing
    (C) hailed...predicting
    (D) negated...anticipating

34. I hoped to -------- the rock wall with relative ease, but a bad ankle sprain at the start forced me to -------- my goal.

    (A) scale...achieve
    (B) ascend...abandon
    (C) trek...improve
    (D) ply...enervate

35. Some worry that social networking sites are -------- to our social lives, and find it -------- that many people have more virtual friends than real ones.

    (A) hazardous...relaxing
    (B) detrimental...unnerving
    (C) beneficial...exciting
    (D) fortunate...scary

36. Though the original Model T Fords were -------- by comparison with modern cars, they were actually more -------- than some cars of the early 1970s.

    (A) wasteful...efficient
    (B) sleek...stylish
    (C) flat...ineffective
    (D) unattractive...resourceful

Go on to the next page ➡

37. Though Ben Stiller movies are usually -------- and easy to follow, his latest film proved to be dreary and --------.

    (A) depressing...unfathomable

    (B) hilarious...visible

    (C) old-fashioned...paranoid

    (D) amusing...opaque

38. William Shakespeare often -------- new phrases and even new words in his work, earning him a reputation as a bold and -------- writer.

    (A) coined...innovative

    (B) faked...productive

    (C) created...loathsome

    (D) analyzed...barbarous

39. Many people claim they don't eat -------- food because it doesn't taste good; they would prefer the food they eat be both healthy and --------.

    (A) perilous...delicious

    (B) nutritious...appetizing

    (C) innocent...unappealing

    (D) excessive...reliable

40. While Sarah viewed snow days as a -------- when they secured her a day out of school, they became more of a -------- when they interfered with her travel plans.

    (A) blessing...chance

    (B) horror...farce

    (C) boon...hindrance

    (D) byproduct...task

STOP. Do not go on until told to do so.

STOP

Section 2
Quantitative Reasoning

37 Questions | **Time: 35 minutes**

Each question is followed by four suggested answers. Read each question and then decide which one of the four suggested answers is best.

Find the row of spaces on your answer document that has the same number as the question. In this row, mark the space having the same letter as the answer you have chosen. You may write in your test booklet.

SAMPLE QUESTIONS: <u>Sample Answer</u>

What is the value of the expression $(4 + 6) \div 2$? Ⓐ Ⓑ ● Ⓓ

(A) 2

(B) 4

(C) 5

(D) 7

The correct answer is 5, so circle C is darkened.

A square has an area of 25cm^2. What is the length of one of its sides? Ⓐ ● Ⓒ Ⓓ

(A) 1 cm

(B) 5 cm

(C) 10 cm

(D) 25 cm

The correct answer is 5, so circle B is darkened.

Go on to the next page ➡

PART TWO — QUANTITATIVE COMPARISONS

All questions in Part Two are quantitative comparisons between the quantities shown in Column A and Column B. Using the information given in each question, compare the quantity in Column A to the quantity in Column B, and choose one of these four answer choices:

(A) The quantity in Column A is greater.
(B) The quantity in Column B is greater.
(C) The two quantities are equal.
(D) The relationship cannot be determined from the information given.

SAMPLE QUESTIONS:

Column A	Column B	Sample Answer
5	$\sqrt{25}$	Ⓐ Ⓑ ● Ⓓ

The quantity in Column A (5) is the same as the quantity in Column B (5), so circle C is darkened.

$x = 6^2 - 3 \times 4$

Column A	Column B	Sample Answer
x	22	● Ⓑ Ⓒ Ⓓ

The quantity in Column A (24) is greater than the quantity in Column B (22), so circle A is darkened.

STOP. Do not go on until told to do so.

STOP

PART ONE – WORD PROBLEMS

Directions: Choose the best answer from the four choices given.

1. The formula for a cylinder's volume is $V = \pi r^2 h$, where r is the cylinder's radius and h is the cylinder's height. If a cylinder has a radius equal to its height h, what is the cylinder's volume in terms of its height?

   (A) $4\pi h$
   (B) πh^3
   (C) $2\pi h^3$
   (D) $16\pi h^3$

2. The diagram below shows a 12" long piece of paper that Samantha folded in half. She made one cut so that when she unfolded the paper, a perfect circle had been cut out.

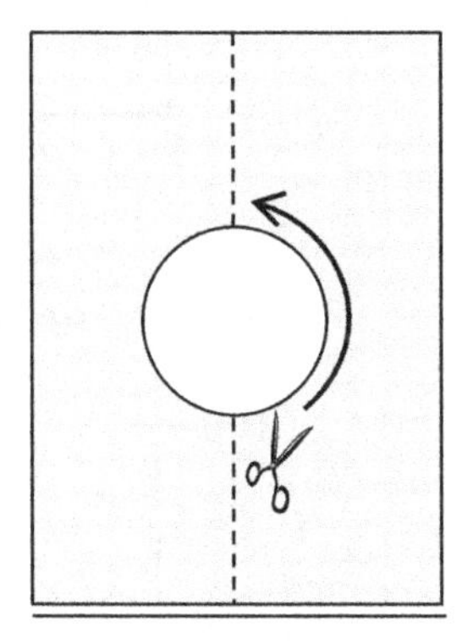

   If the circle's diameter measures $\frac{1}{3}$ of the length of the paper, what was the length of the cut she made?

   (A) 2 in.
   (B) 4 in.
   (C) 2π in.
   (D) 3π in.

3. The irregular polygon below has sides of unequal lengths.

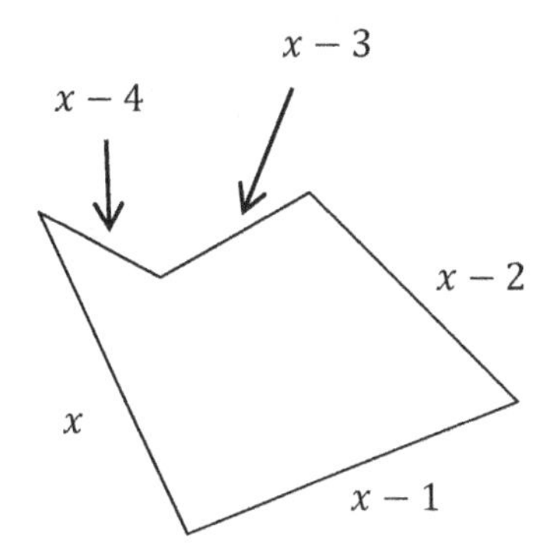

   If the polygon's total perimeter is 20, what is the value of x?

   (A) 6
   (B) 5
   (C) 4
   (D) 2

4. If $y^{-2} = (x-2)^{\frac{1}{2}}$, then which expression is equal to x?

   (A) $y^2 + 2$
   (B) $\frac{2}{y^4}$
   (C) $2 - y^{-2}$
   (D) $\frac{1}{y^4} + 2$

5. Which of the following expressions is equivalent to $\left(\frac{2^4}{4^2}\right)^2$?

   (A) $(2)^{\frac{1}{2}}$
   (B) 4^0
   (C) $(2)^{-\frac{1}{2}}$
   (D) 4^{-2}

Go on to the next page ➡

6. If the sum of all integers from 600 to 800, inclusive, is w, what is the average value of all of these integers?

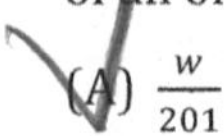

(A) $\frac{w}{201}$

(B) $\frac{w^2}{101 \times 100}$

(C) $(w - 101)^2$

(D) $201 \times w$

7. The rectangle below has an area of $7m^2$.

$Area = 7m^2$

Note: figure not to scale.

If all sides of the rectangle are integers, which of the following could be the perimeter of the rectangle?

(A) 49

(B) 28

(C) 16

(D) 12

8. Luisa is thinking of a prime number that is greater than 8 and less than 30. If Elizabeth randomly guesses one number that fits this description, what is her probability of guessing Luisa's number?

(A) $\frac{1}{29}$

(B) $\frac{1}{22}$

(C) $\frac{1}{9}$

(D) $\frac{1}{6}$

9. Franklin was simmering 10 cups of soup at a constant temperature of 95°F. He then added 2 cups of broth, which had a temperature of 95°F. Which graph best represents the temperature of his soup as a function of time?

(A)

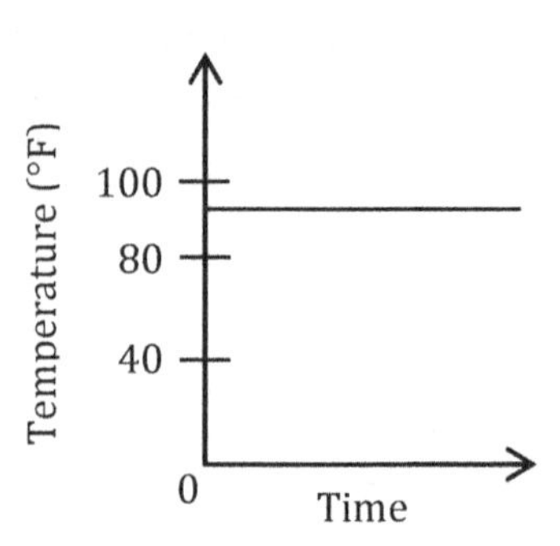

(B)

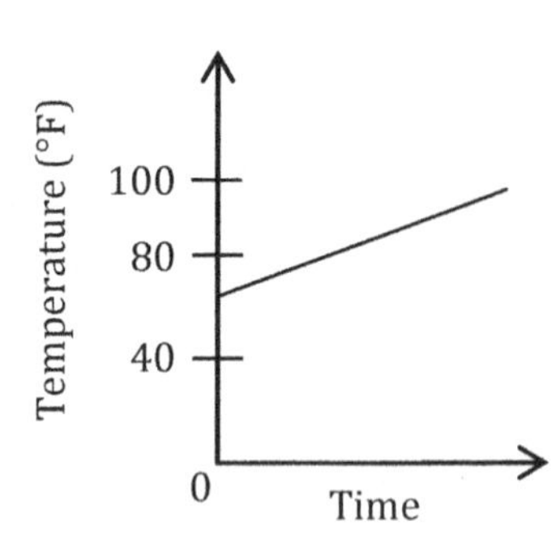

(C)

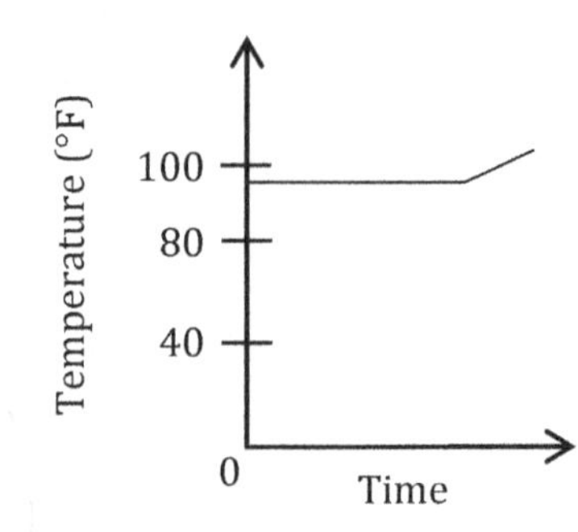

(D)

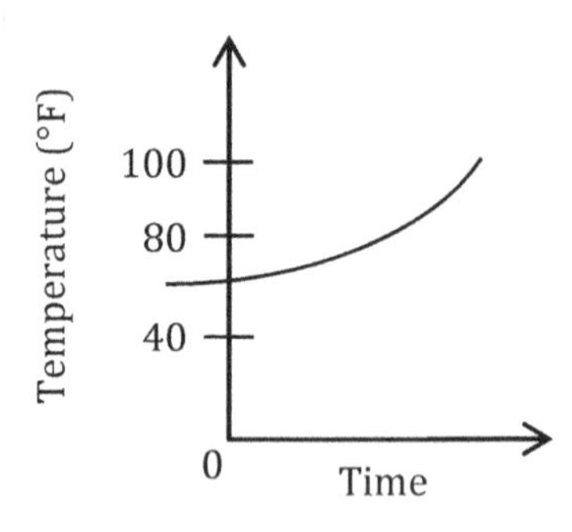

Go on to the next page ➡

10. If $5 :: 8 = 5^2 - 8$, what is the value of $7 :: 3$?

(A) 21
(B) 40
(C) 46
(D) 49

11. The two triangles below are similar. Triangle B's sides are proportionally $\frac{2}{3}$ the length of Triangle A's.

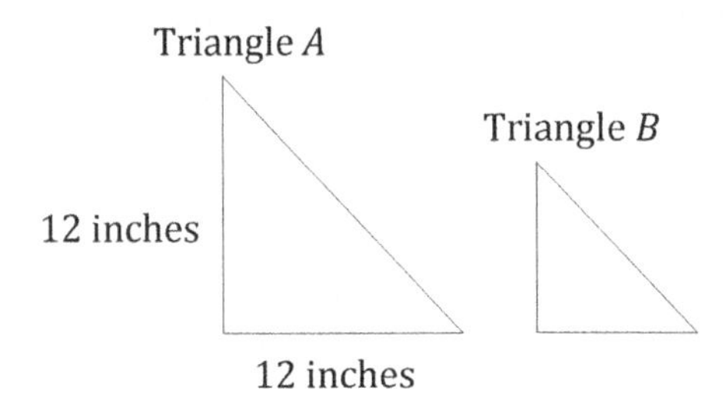

What is the ratio of Triangle A's area to Triangle B's area?

(A) 3 to 5
(B) 2 to 1
(C) 2 to 3
(D) 9 to 4

12. The stem-and-leaf plot below shows the results of 20 students' test scores in Mrs. Louis's class.

Stem	Leaf
10	0 0
9	9 8 8 5 2
8	9 7 6 4 4 4 3 0
7	3 3 2 1 0

Mrs. Louis decided to boost the students' test scores by increasing each score by 10%. What was the range of the data after this boost?

(A) 27
(B) 30
(C) 33
(D) 84

13. If u is a positive integer and $(t + u)^2 = t^2 + 26t + u^2$, what is the value of u?

(A) 3
(B) 13
(C) 26
(D) 169

14. The variables a and b are both positive integers. If $a > b$ and $ab = 9$, what is the value of $a^2 - b^2$?

(A) 80
(B) 9
(C) 0
(D) -80

15. The shaded right triangle is attached to a square by its hypotenuse, as shown in the figure below. The perimeter of the square is x cm.

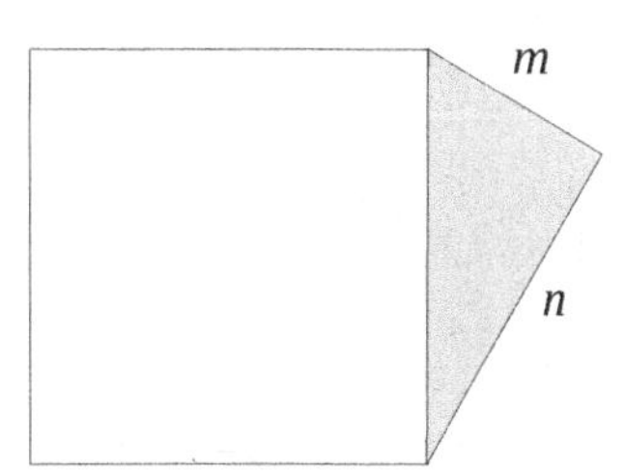

What is the value of $m^2 + n^2$?

(A) $x - 4$
(B) $x^2 \times 4$
(C) $\left(\frac{x}{4}\right)^2$
(D) $\left(\frac{x}{16}\right)^2$

16. A square has an area of A. If the length of each side is decreased by 50%, what is the square's new area, in terms of A?

(A) $4A$
(B) $2A$
(C) $\frac{1}{2}A$
(D) $\frac{A}{4}$

Go on to the next page ➡

17. Use the chart below to answer the question.

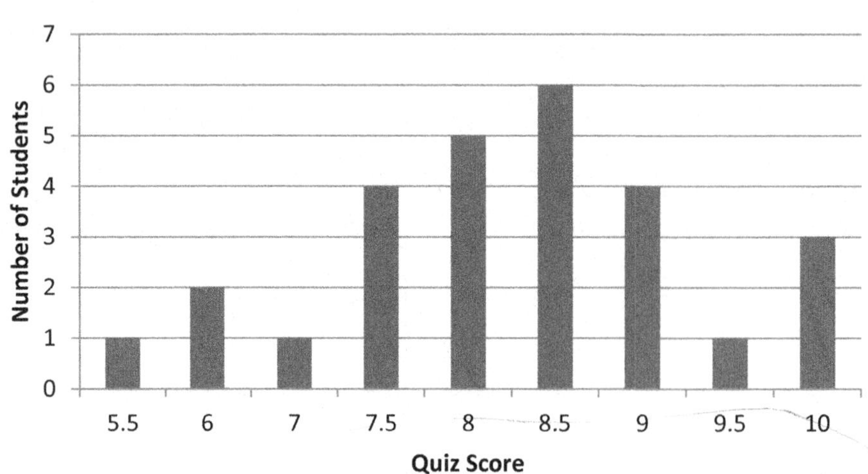

One student's quiz has not yet been graded. Which of the following quiz grades would cause the data's median to change the most?

(A) 7.5
(B) 8.5
(C) 9.5
(D) 10

---

18. Use the graph below to answer the question.

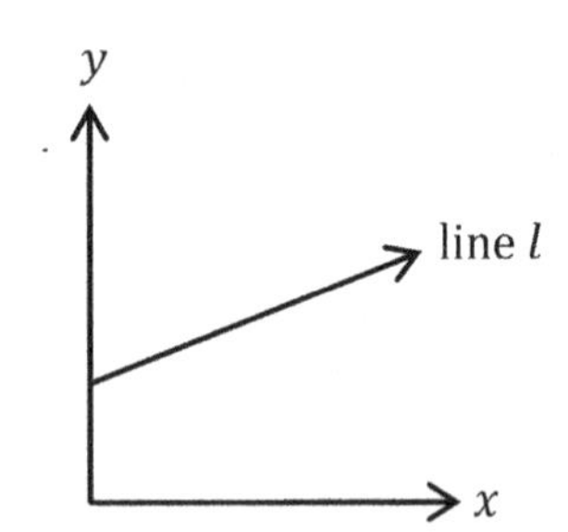

Line k is perpendicular to line l. Line k's slope could NOT be which of the following type of number?

(A) A composite number
(B) A positive integer
(C) A prime number
(D) A rational number

19. Which of the following expressions is equivalent to the expression $x^2 - 4$?

(A) $(x + \sqrt{2})(x - \sqrt{2})$
(B) $(x + 2)(x - 2)$
(C) $(x - \sqrt{2})^2$
(D) $(x + 2i)(x - 2i)$

Go on to the next page ➡

20. A cube is shown.

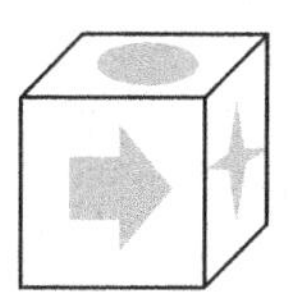

Which of the figures is a possible net for the cube?

(A)

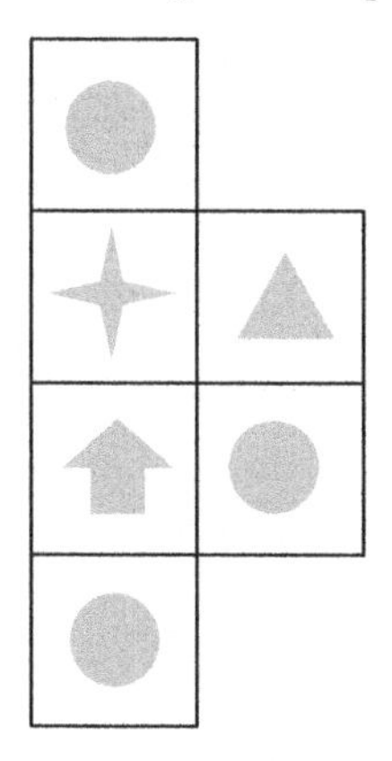

(C)

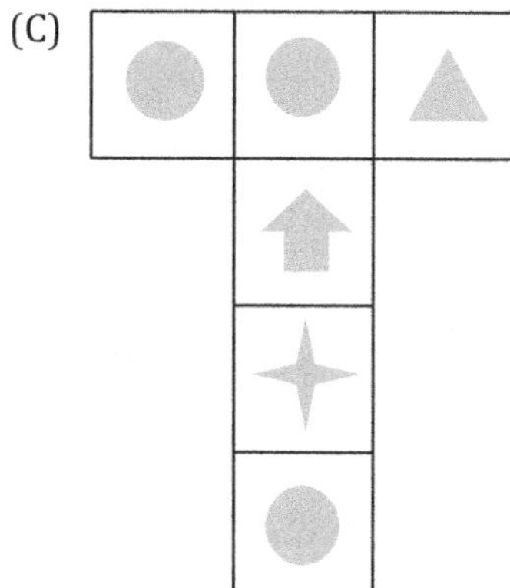

(B)

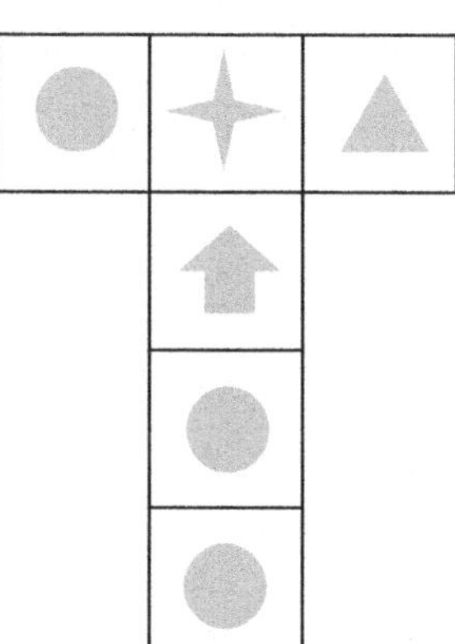

(D)

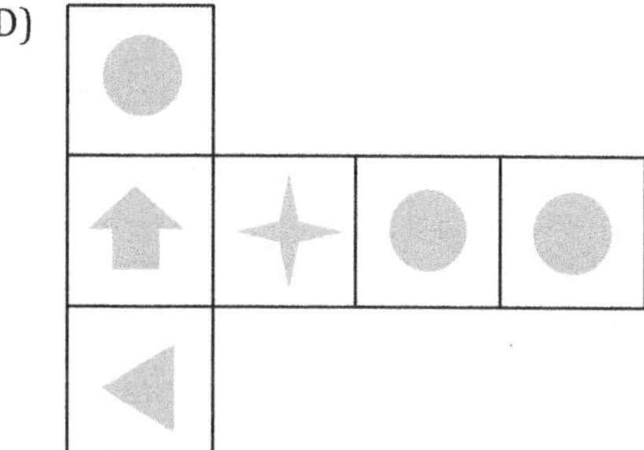

Go on to the next page ➡

PART TWO – QUANTITATIVE COMPARISONS

Directions: Using the information given in each question, compare the quantity in column A to the quantity in Column B. All questions in Part Two have these answer choices:

(A) The quantity in Column A is greater.

(B) The quantity in Column B is greater.

(C) The two quantities are equal.

(D) The relationship cannot be determined from the information given.

The two rectangles shown below are similar.

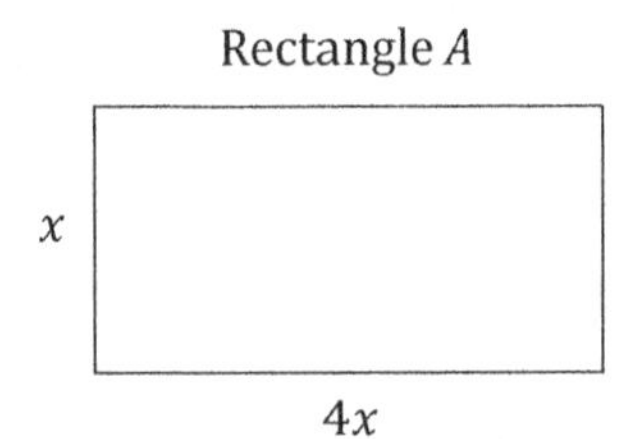

Rectangle B

$\frac{3}{2}x$

Note: figure not to scale

	Column A	Column B
21.	The area of rectangle B	$8x^2$

The diagram below shows the results of a survey that asked 860 people about their pets.

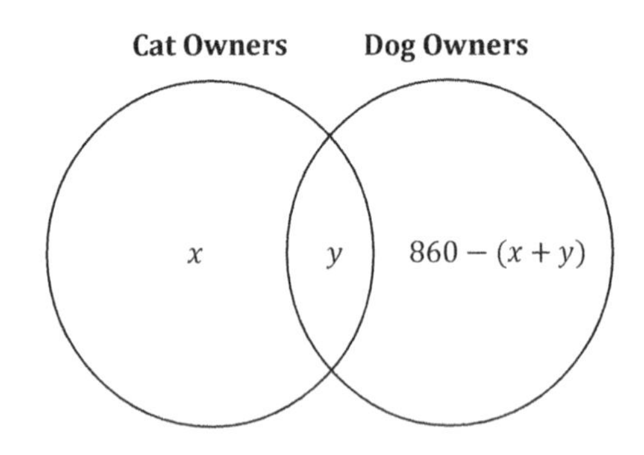

	Column A	Column B
22.	The number of people who own a cat	The number of people who own a dog

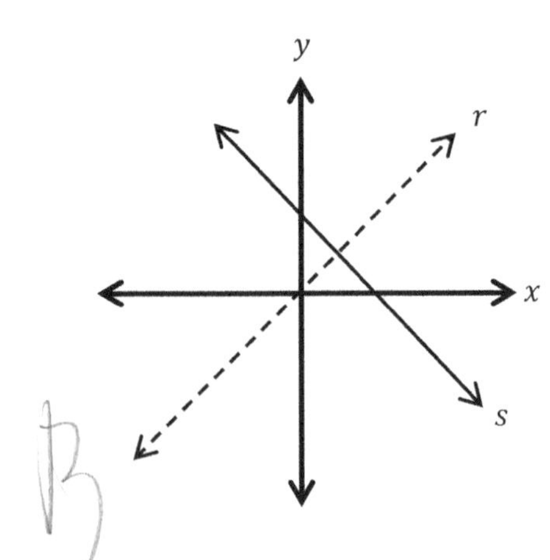

Line r is the graph of $2x + b$. Line s is perpendicular to line r.

	Column A	Column B
23.	-2	The slope of line s

Go on to the next page ➡

ANSWER CHOICES FOR ALL QUESTIONS ON THIS PAGE:

(A) The quantity in Column A is greater.
(B) The quantity in Column B is greater.
(C) The two quantities are equal.
(D) The relationship cannot be determined from the information given.

	Column A	Column B
24.	25×20	26×19

	Column A	Column B
25.	The sum of all prime numbers greater than 35 and less than 43	The sum of all prime numbers less than 23.

$[\blacklozenge]p = 2(p - 3) - 5$

	Column A	Column B
26.	$[\blacklozenge]2$	-3

	Column A	Column B
27.	30% of 20	20% of 30

y is a positive integer whole number

	Column A	Column B
28.	y^2	 $\left(\frac{1}{y}\right)^{-3}$

The circular target below has a diameter of 8 feet. A square section of the target with side lengths of $\sqrt{\pi}$ feet has been shaded in.

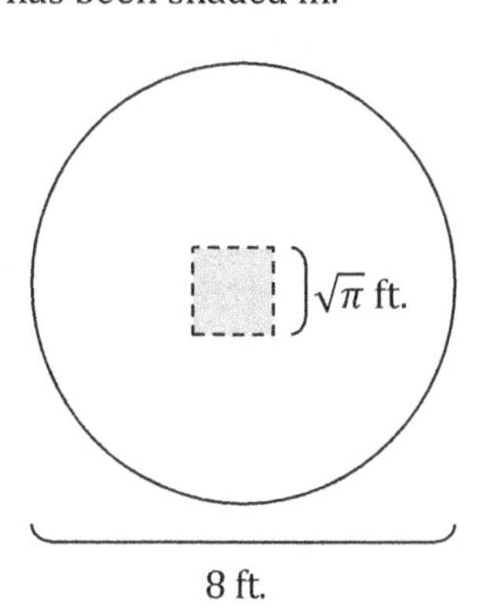

A beanbag that has been randomly tossed lands on the circular target.

	Column A	Column B
29.	The probability that the beanbag lands within the shaded square	$\frac{1}{16}$

Pete has ten carrots and one piece of celery in his lunch. He is randomly selecting vegetables to eat one at a time.

	Column A	Column B
30.	The probability that he eats one carrot and then the piece of celery	The probability that he eats the piece of celery and then one carrot

Go on to the next page ➡

ANSWER CHOICES FOR ALL QUESTIONS ON THIS PAGE:

(A) The quantity in Column A is greater.
(B) The quantity in Column B is greater.
(C) The two quantities are equal.
(D) The relationship cannot be determined from the information given.

Two cylinders are shown below. Cylinder B is twice as tall as Cylinder A, but is one-half as wide. The formula for the volume of a cylinder is $V = \pi r^2 h$.

Cylinder A Cylinder B

Note: Figures not drawn to scale.

	Column A	Column B
31.	The volume of Cylinder A	The volume of Cylinder B

$$x^3 - 12x^2 + 35x = 0$$

	Column A	Column B
32.	x	4

6% of the audience members, or 10 people, enjoyed a certain play.

	Column A	Column B
33.	The total number of audience members	100

Use the figure below to answer the question.

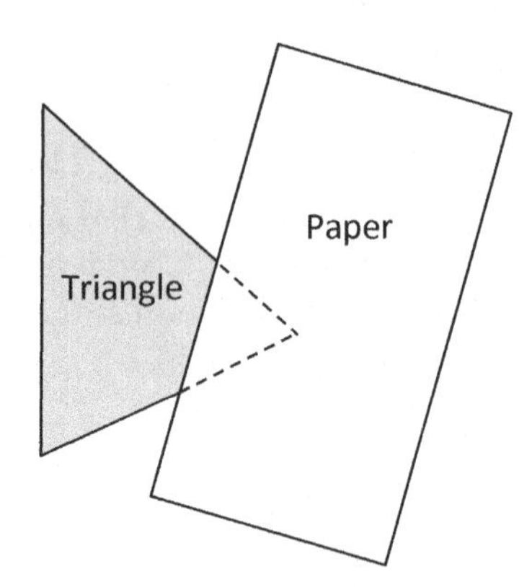

A triangle is partially covered by a piece of paper so that only the shaded portion is visible.

	Column A	Column B
34.	The sum of the interior angles of the original triangle	The sum of the interior angles of the shaded region

	Column A	Column B
35.	The surface area of a 10 cm × 10 cm × 10 cm cube	The surface area of a 10 cm × 5 cm × 20 cm rectangular prism

$(e^2 + f^2) = 13$ and $ef = 6$

	Column A	Column B
36.	$(e + f)^2$	$2ef$

Go on to the next page ➡

ANSWER CHOICES FOR ALL QUESTIONS ON THIS PAGE:

(A) The quantity in Column A is greater.
(B) The quantity in Column B is greater.
(C) The two quantities are equal.
(D) The relationship cannot be determined from the information given.

Use the histogram below to answer the question.

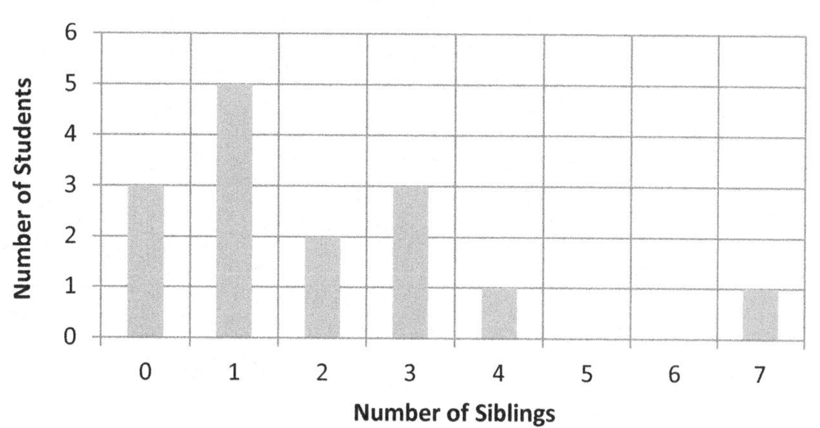

	Column A	Column B
37.	The median of the data.	The mode of the data.

STOP. Do not go on until told to do so.

STOP

Section 3
Reading Comprehension

36 Questions

Time: 35 minutes

This section contains six short reading passages. Each passage is followed by six questions based on its content. Answer the questions following each passage on the basis of what is stated or implied in that passage. You may write in your test booklet.

STOP. Do not go on until told to do so.

STOP

Questions 1–6

1 As a child, I had the good fortune to be
2 given all the spare parts and broken devices
3 that I could have desired, which were the
4 surpluses of my father's business. To a curious
5 child, of course, nearly any object can become
6 an object of play- but the complex and
7 interesting things that were cast off from my
8 father's shop were exceptional toys, and superb
9 materials for experimentation.
10 It won't be a surprise that I began my
11 experiments mainly by disassembling things
12 and leaving them in a pile. After a while, I
13 began to have some luck in putting things back
14 together. But since the devices were broken
15 already when I received them, there was little I
16 could do to confirm the soundness of my work
17 but to see that they looked right, and perhaps
18 to spin with my finger what should properly be
19 spun by a motor. Then came a day when I
20 cracked open a simple electric motor which
21 had been extracted from a fan brought in for
22 repair: the motor wouldn't run, was deemed
23 dead, and was handed off to me for my play. I
24 had opened up similar devices before, and had
25 a vague idea of their operation, although I did
26 not know the names of all the parts as I do now.
27 An electric motor contains several
28 magnets arranged around a central rotor,
29 which holds an electromagnet. At the base of
30 the rotor is a "commutator," which is a sort of
31 spinning switch. Several metal brushes make
32 contact with the commutator, and complete a
33 circuit which powers the electromagnet on the
34 rotor. When powered, the electromagnet is
35 alternately repelled and attracted by the
36 magnets around it. The rotor is thus kept in
37 constant motion so long as the electromagnet is
38 supplied with electricity.
39 In the motor which I had just opened,
40 one of the metallic brushes which make contact
41 with the commutator (and thereby supply
42 power to the electromagnet in the rotor and
43 make the whole process work) had somehow
44 come to be bent away from its intended
45 position. Because of the dislocation of this vital
46 component, the circuit could not be completed
47 and the electromagnet could not receive
48 power. All there was for me to do was to bend
49 the brush back into place, and attach the motor
50 to a battery- and it whirred to life there in front
51 of me! I excitedly presented the work to my
52 father, was congratulated, and was rewarded
53 with an apple tart and an invitation thereafter
54 to come and help out in the shop with simple
55 repairs.

Go on to the next page ➡

1. Which sentence best summarizes this passage?
   (A) An electric motor has a part called a "commutator," which is a very important part that is necessary for the motor to function.
   (B) Although the narrator needed to repair an electric motor, he was frustrated because he only had broken devices to work with.
   (C) The narrator was allowed to play with broken machines as a child, and after fixing an electric motor was given congratulations and rewards.
   (D) The passage lists the parts of electric motors, and provides basic instructions for repairing them when damaged.

2. Based on the passage, we can conclude that an electromagnet
   (A) needs to be supplied with electricity in order to function properly.
   (B) is a component used to power fans.
   (C) will continue to spin out of control if its circuit is broken.
   (D) is a very valuable component which should not be lightly discarded.

3. As it is used in line 45, "dislocation" most nearly means
   (A) annihilation
   (B) misplacement
   (C) circulation
   (D) correction

4. The role of the metallic brushes in an electric motor is to
   (A) hold the commutator firmly in place.
   (B) keep the internal components clean.
   (C) complete a circuit in the motor.
   (D) safely discharge excess electricity.

5. Based on information in the passage, which of the following statements about the narrator's father is most likely to be true?
   (A) The narrator's father was too busy to pay much attention to his son, and so the narrator was left to play alone.
   (B) The narrator's father spent much of his free time teaching his son to repair broken machinery.
   (C) The narrator's father was too poor to afford real toys, so he gave his son junk to play with instead.
   (D) The narrator's father operated a business which repaired a lot of broken mechanical devices.

6. The purpose of the third paragraph is to
   (A) tell the story of how the narrator fixed an electric motor.
   (B) explain how the narrator came to possess and electric motor.
   (C) add details which help to support the narrator's argument.
   (D) describe how an electric motor operates.

Go on to the next page ➡

Questions 7–12

1 It is common today to read about the
2 revolutionary nature of the Internet. It doesn't
3 take much exposure to the claims of the tech
4 crowd to see that just about every aspect of our
5 lives has purportedly been changed
6 fundamentally and forever by the advent of the
7 Web. But how fundamental have the changes
8 brought about by the Internet really been?
9 The first thing one should know when
10 considering the proposition that the Internet
11 has changed the world is that, as of 2012,
12 Internet users only make up a little more than a
13 third of the world population. However
14 revolutionary the changes may be for that
15 networked minority, most of the world
16 continues to drudge on without the Web.
17 And to those of us who are online, much
18 of what the Internet brings is not clearly new,
19 and some of it is not even clearly useful. Online
20 shopping is only a quicker, more convenient
21 version of mail-order shopping. Searching for
22 information online is a quicker version of
23 searching a library, but the credibility of online
24 sources is often questionable. Communicating
25 online is hardly an improvement at all over
26 previous technologies: it may be nearly instant,
27 but so are phone calls and radio
28 communication- and they've been around for a
29 century! And online communication certainly
30 doesn't provide a clear benefit to our social
31 lives: studies suggest that as we make more
32 and more friends online, we have fewer and
33 fewer in real life- and real friends are worth far
34 more than nominal Internet "friends."
35 The Internet is certainly a convenience,
36 which enables us to do more quickly many of
37 the things which we have always done, without
38 so much as leaving our chairs. But it is not
39 without its downsides, and ultimately it is still
40 only a convenience: it is not the end of human
41 progress, the final stage of history, or the
42 zenith of human achievement. The sense of the
43 all-encompassing importance of the Internet is
44 merely a symptom of our newfound reliance on
45 this great modern convenience, and will seem
46 as quaint and misguided to our descendants as
47 the industrial-age fantasy that industrialization
48 would free humanity from the demands of
49 labor, to live in endless leisure and abundance.

Go on to the next page ➡

7. The main purpose of this passage is to
   (A) persuade the reader that the Internet isn't actually a revolutionary invention.
   (B) provide an unbiased overview of how the Internet has affected our lives.
   (C) opine that online friends are not worth as much as real friends.
   (D) discuss pre-internet technologies that had functions now carried out by the Internet.

8. The passage implies that information in a library
   (A) is easier to access than online information.
   (B) is actually about as easy to search through as online information.
   (C) is more credible than information on the Internet.
   (D) is less likely to have a negative impact on your social life.

9. Lines 29-34 suggest that online friendships
   (A) are more numerous than in-person friendships.
   (B) are only beneficial to certain types of people.
   (C) shouldn't be considered as real friendships.
   (D) often cause harm to your in-person friendships.

10. Which of the following sentences restates one of the author's main points?
    (A) It's unfair to most of the world to use the Internet as a primary form of communication.
    (B) Many of the things we do on the Internet can also be done without the Internet.
    (C) People who spend too much time online will lose all of their friends.
    (D) Although it's convenient, the Internet is not as revolutionary as industrialization.

11. Which best describes the organization of this passage?
    (A) A question is posed, some evidence is discussed, and a conclusion is clearly stated only after providing evidence.
    (B) A fact is stated, some questions are asked about the fact, and answers are provided to each question in turn.
    (C) The passage offers evidence on two sides of an issue, leaving it to the reader to draw their own conclusions.
    (D) The passage provides evidence in favor of one side of an argument, without considering any counter-evidence.

12. As it is used in line 5, the word "purportedly" most nearly means
    (A) undeniably.
    (B) supposedly.
    (C) unfortunately.
    (D) similarly.

Go on to the next page ➡

Questions 13–18

Scrimshaw is an art of creating delicate engravings on the teeth and bones of whales, or the tusks of walruses, and the artisan who practices scrimshaw is called a scrimshander.

The practice began on whaling ships between 1745 and 1759. It derived from the practice of creating common tools on-board the ship using the bones of whales, which were abundant and easily accessible on whaling ships. Whalers had more free time than other sailors of the period - and so, at times when others might have been working, whalers needed a hobby. Using simple needles, they began to etch designs and pictures into the teeth and bones of whales, and to highlight their engravings with dark pigments- often soot, or tobacco juice.

The practice of scrimshaw expanded as the market for whale teeth grew, reaching its peak in the middle of the 19th century. The market declined as the whaling industry waned in the latter part of the 1800s, and in 1976 an international treaty called the Convention on International Trade in Endangered Species of Wild Fauna and Flora, or CITES, was signed- severely restricting trade in the products of whaling, or other activities that threatened endangered species. While it is still legal to trade in the products of whales which were harvested before the treaty, no whale teeth harvested since the signing of the treaty may legally be traded in most parts of the world. Today, as a result, great care must be taken to acquire only legal whale teeth, and the practice of scrimshaw is much less widespread- but the value of antique scrimshaw has increased considerably.

Go on to the next page ➡

13. The main purpose of this passage is to
    (A) explain why Scrimshaw is now a rare art form.
    (B) criticize the CITES treaty for restricting trade.
    (C) describe the history of Scrimshaw.
    (D) explain how Scrimshaw is produced.

14. The purpose of the second paragraph (lines 5-17) is to
    (A) show why whale teeth provided the best material for scrimshanders.
    (B) describe the wealth and leisure enjoyed by whalers.
    (C) foreshadow the end of the art of scrimshaw.
    (D) inform the reader about the origins of scrimshaw.

15. We can infer from the passage that by 1976
    (A) the market for whale teeth had already disappeared.
    (B) the whales traditionally hunted by whalers had become endangered species.
    (C) whalers had generally found other ways to entertain themselves than scrimshaw.
    (D) scrimshanders were primarily using walrus tusks rather than whale teeth.

16. Care must be taken when trading in scrimshaw because
    (A) the pigments used by early scrimshanders are not as durable as the more modern pigments.
    (B) walrus tusks are significantly more brittle than whale teeth.
    (C) the market for scrimshaw is constantly growing, even though the supply of whale teeth has been restricted.
    (D) it is illegal in many places to trade whale teeth harvested after 1976.

17. According to the passage, whalers originally chose the teeth and bones of whales for their carvings because
    (A) the growing market for whale teeth made them a valuable commodity.
    (B) they had easy access to large quantities of those materials.
    (C) whalers had too much free time.
    (D) teeth and bones could be easily dyed with tobacco and soot.

18. Which best describes the effect that the CITES treaty on the trade in scrimshaw?
    (A) The CITES treaty banned the sale of scrimshaw, but still allowed scrimshanders to make new scrimshaw.
    (B) When CITES was passed, the scrimshaw market finally reached its peak, and then declined as the whaling industry shrank.
    (C) CITES imposed new restrictions on the trade of new whale teeth, but did not prohibit the sale of antique scrimshaw.
    (D) Scrimshaw was banned under CITES, although raw whale teeth could still be harvested and traded.

Go on to the next page ➡

Questions 19–24

National Forests are largely forest and woodland areas owned by the federal government and managed by the United States Forest Service, part of the United States Department of Agriculture. Land management of these areas focuses on conservation, timber harvesting, livestock grazing, watershed protection, wildlife, and recreation. Unlike national parks and other federal lands managed by the National Park Service, extraction of natural resources from national forests is sanctioned, and in many cases encouraged.

The National Forest system was created by the Land Revision Act of 1891. It was the result of concerted action by Los Angeles-area businessmen and property owners who were concerned about the harm being done to the watershed of the San Gabriel Mountains by ranchers and miners. Before the passage of the act, it was common practice in the area to burn down large swathes of forest, to make room for grazing land or for other purposes. Such "burned over" lands are vulnerable to dramatic soil erosion, and the fire-damaged and diminished soil was able to absorb and hold less water.

Under the Land Revision Act, the president was granted the authority to set aside lands which could otherwise have been cheaply purchased from the federal government under the Homestead Act and other laws. Because extraction of resources and other activity in US Forest Lands could be managed by the Forest Service, the damage from land use could be limited.

There are, however, still conflicts between timber and mining companies, environmentalists, and recreational users of National Forest land- such as hunters, campers, and hikers- over the use of National Forest land. These conflicts center on land use, logging practices, mining laws, and road-building in National Forests.

The task of the Forest Service is to balance the interests of all the users of National Forest lands, and to create sustainable management plans for forests which will allow the public to continue to enjoy all that the forests have to offer for generations to come.

Go on to the next page ➡

19. We can infer from the passage that before the Land Revision Act

    (A) the majority of privately owned forests had already been burned down.

    (B) miners and ranchers were able to steal federal lands for their own use.

    (C) other laws required the government to sell some of its lands to private buyers.

    (D) land use practices were much more responsible, and safeguarded the soil and water.

20. According to the passage, the creation of the National Forest system was motivated mainly by

    (A) the potential for revenues from sustainable logging and hunting.

    (B) the needs of recreational hikers, hunters, and campers.

    (C) the need to offer affordable lands for sale under the Homestead Act.

    (D) damage being done to the environment by harmful land use.

21. The purpose of lines 20-27 is to

    (A) persuade the reader that miners and ranchers cannot be good stewards of the environment.

    (B) exaggerate the harms that were caused by some uses of natural resources.

    (C) describe the mission and importance of the US Forest Service.

    (D) describe the harmful practices that prompted the passage of the Land Revision Act.

22. With regard to the conflicts that still exist over the appropriate use of National Forest lands (lines 37-44), the author appears to

    (A) side exclusively with the environmentalists, hikers, and campers.

    (B) strongly favor the position of the timber and mining companies.

    (C) support the Forest Service's mission of balancing competing interests.

    (D) support a change in the Forest Service's current policies.

23. As it is used in line 12, the word "sanctioned" most nearly means

    (A) excluded.

    (B) purchased.

    (C) permitted.

    (D) required.

24. With which of the following sentences would the author of the passage most likely agree?

    (A) With good land management, natural resources can be exploited without causing excessive harm to the environment.

    (B) National Forest lands are an underutilized resource, and the Forest Service should allow more exploitation of natural resources on federal lands.

    (C) The Forest Service is a much more important government agency than the National Park Service.

    (D) Logging and mining should not be allowed in national forest lands, which should be mainly reserved for recreational use.

Go on to the next page ➡

Questions 25–30

1 Jean Piaget was a psychologist and
2 philosopher best known for his work with
3 children. Piaget was interested in how people
4 develop as they get older, and more specifically
5 with how they perceive the world, and learn in
6 different ways, as they grow up.
7 Early in his career, Piaget helped to score
8 intelligence tests administered in a school
9 where he was employed, and while scoring
10 them he noticed that there were differences
11 between the results that younger children
12 achieved and the results attained by adults. At
13 the time, the prevailing belief in psychology
14 was that children thought in basically the same
15 way as adults, but that they were simply less
16 competent- so you would expect for a child not
17 to do as well as an adult on a test of
18 intelligence. But there were particular types of
19 mistakes which adults did not make, and which
20 children would consistently make. To Piaget,
21 that suggested more than just different levels
22 of intelligence: that suggested that children
23 were thinking in fundamentally different ways
24 from adults.
25 Piaget would go on to conduct a number
26 of revealing experiments with children of
27 various ages that showed the ways in which
28 their perception of the world changed as they
29 grew. Based on his observations, Piaget defined
30 a series of stages of development in children,
31 during which their perceptions of the world
32 change in significant ways. For this work, he is
33 regarded by some as the father of
34 Developmental Psychology, the field of
35 psychology concerned with the growth and
36 development of human minds.
37 Piaget's work hasn't survived without
38 criticism: many of the distinctions between the
39 stages may not be as clear as Piaget proposed,
40 and some researchers have contended that his
41 experimental results are the product of
42 phenomena other than his proposed stages of
43 development. But Piaget's work has
44 nonetheless been profoundly influential.
45 Generations of psychologists and educators
46 have studied Piaget, and his thinking has
47 helped to shape the way that school curricula
48 are designed, the ways in which psychologists
49 work with children, and the advice that some
50 parenting experts give on raising children.

Go on to the next page ➡

25. This passage is mainly concerned with

    (A) discussing the career and legacy of Jean Piaget.

    (B) exploring the implications of Piaget's theories for teachers and psychologists.

    (C) describing the theories of Jean Piaget.

    (D) providing a critical view of Piaget's work.

26. As it is used in line 13, the word "prevailing" most nearly means

    (A) victorious.

    (B) dominant.

    (C) singular.

    (D) improbable.

27. Which of the following statements is supported by information in the passage?

    (A) Piaget's ideas about psychology are no longer relevant, but he is still notable as a philosopher.

    (B) Psychologists and teachers continue to resist Piaget's ideas, but have been unable to disprove them.

    (C) The children that Piaget worked with developed very well, and continue to serve as a model for students and educators today.

    (D) Ideas about development have changed somewhat since Piaget's time, but his work remains important.

28. Which of the following questions would probably have been LEAST relevant to Piaget's studies?

    (A) Why do some adults do better than other adults on IQ tests?

    (B) Are there some problems that young children solve faster than older ones?

    (C) Do adults learn new activities more quickly than children?

    (D) At what age can children solve simple problems with algebra?

29. Which of the following words could replace "competent" in line 16 without changing the meaning of the sentence?

    (A) appropriate

    (B) adequate

    (C) credentialed

    (D) capable

30. Piaget first began to notice fundamental differences in the way that children and adults think when

    (A) he helped to create the first intelligence tests for children and adults.

    (B) he realized that the prevailing beliefs in psychology may be wrong.

    (C) he was helping to score intelligence tests administered to adults and children.

    (D) he conducted experiments with children of various ages.

Go on to the next page ➡

Questions 31–36

Salt is often used as a de-icing agent on roads and sidewalks because a solution of salt and water has a lower freezing point than pure water. The ice exchanges molecules with the salt, creating a solution, and because this solution has a lower freezing point than pure water, the ice often melts. If the temperature is very cold, however, the ice may remain solid. In such cases, sand is spread over the surface of the ice in order to maintain traction, rather than trying to melt the ice.

Salt is also added to ice to make cold brine. The chemical reaction that occurs as the salt melts the ice actually reduces the temperature of the solution, resulting in liquid water which is colder than the normal freezing point of water. This effect is used when making ice cream: a container of flavored cream is frozen by submerging it in cold brine while stirring, although care is taken to avoid letting the brine mix with the cream.

It is widely believed that salt also lowers the boiling point of water, which would cause water to come to a boil more quickly when heated. However, salt actually has the opposite effect: adding salt to water increases its boiling point, meaning that salted water must reach a higher temperature than unsalted water before it begins to boil. This is a very small effect, however. Almost twelve teaspoons of salt would be required to increase the boiling point of an ounce of water by one degree Fahrenheit. Thus, the amount of salt that is typically used in cooking probably has no real impact on the speed at which water boils.

It does, however, affect the flavor of the food. Salt has been used in food preparation for as long as humans have been keeping record, both because it can enhance the flavors of otherwise bland or bitter foods, and because it is a natural preservative. This is because salt draws in moisture, dehydrating foods treated with generous applications of salt. Such dried foods are less hospitable to the bacteria that cause the decomposition of fresh, moist foods, and can thus be stored for long periods of time without decay.

This process of using salt to preserve foods is called curing, and requires a concentration of salt of nearly 20% to be effective. Curing is used especially often to preserve meat or fish, but certain vegetables such as cabbage can also be stored this way. The primary ingredient used in curing foods is simple table salt, along with other compounds such as nitrates, nitrites, and sugar. Salt is sometimes also used in smaller doses in other forms of food preservation, such as pickling.

Go on to the next page ➡

31. People often spread salt on icy streets and sidewalks in order to

    (A) generate heat that will melt the ice.
    (B) increase traction.
    (C) melt the ice by lowering its freezing point.
    (D) warn drivers of icy conditions.

32. Adding a pinch of salt to a large pot of water would most likely

    (A) cause the water to boil more quickly.
    (B) cause the water to boil more slowly.
    (C) have little impact on the water's boiling point.
    (D) be enough to cure any meat in the water.

33. In line 13 the word "brine" most nearly means

    (A) a solution of salt and water.
    (B) frozen saltwater.
    (C) boiling saltwater.
    (D) a solution of sand and ice.

34. The author's style in this passage could best be described as

    (A) argumentative.
    (B) expository.
    (C) narrative.
    (D) condescending.

35. This passage is primarily about

    (A) the properties and uses of salt.
    (B) how salt is used to melt ice.
    (C) how salt interacts with water.
    (D) salt's use in food preparation.

36. The function of the third paragraph (lines 22–35) is to

    (A) argue that salt lowers the boiling point of water.
    (B) discuss salt's use as a natural preservative.
    (C) describe salt's impact on the boiling point of water.
    (D) explain the chemical composition of salt.

STOP. Do not go on until told to do so.

STOP

SECTION 4

Mathematics Achievement

47 Questions **Time: 40 minutes**

Each question is followed by four suggested answers. Read each question and then decide which one of the four suggested answers is best.

Find the row of spaces on your answer document that has the same number as the question. In this row, mark the space having the same letter as the answer you have chosen. You may write in your test booklet.

SAMPLE QUESTION:

Sample Answer

If $a = 3$, what is the value $a^2 + (3 \times 4) \div 6$?

Ⓐ ● Ⓒ Ⓓ

(A) 3.5

(B) 11

(C) 14.5

(D) 20

The correct answer is 11, so circle B is darkened.

STOP. Do not go on until told to do so. STOP

1. Which number has the most unique prime factors?

   (A) 15
   (B) 17
   (C) 27
   (D) 43

2. If $y = 2$ and $\frac{xy}{x-y^2} = 0$, then which of the following could be a value of x?

   (A) y^2
   (B) $2y$
   (C) $2 - y$
   (D) $y^2 - 2$

3. How many millimeters are in 0.345km?

   (A) 345 mm
   (B) 3.45×10^3mm
   (C) 3.45×10^5mm
   (D) 3.45×10^6mm

4. $\sqrt{-36} =$

   (A) $6i$
   (B) $-6i$
   (C) 6
   (D) -6

5. There are 3 blue marbles, 5 red marbles, and 7 yellow marbles. Shania is randomly removing marbles from the bag and giving them to her brother. What is the probability that she gives her brother first a blue marble and then a red marble?

   (A) $\frac{1}{15}$
   (B) $\frac{1}{14}$
   (C) $\frac{1}{7}$
   (D) $\frac{8}{15}$

6. At Frank's bakery, a batch of cupcakes requires 12 eggs and 32 cups of flour. If Frank wants to scale down this recipe and make cupcakes at home with 3 eggs, how many cups of flour should he use?

   (A) 4
   (B) 8
   (C) $\frac{32}{3}$
   (D) 20

7. One-fifth of 1.6 plus one-tenth of 3.2 equals

   (A) 0.32.
   (B) 0.64.
   (C) 1.28.
   (D) 4.8.

8. The formula for the volume of a sphere is $V = \frac{4}{3}\pi r^3$. Sphere A has a radius of 2cm and Sphere B has a radius of 4cm. How many times greater is the volume of Sphere B than the volume of Sphere A?

   (A) 2
   (B) $\frac{16}{3}$
   (C) 8
   (D) $\frac{32}{3}$

9. Jen's office is 30km away from her house. On the way to the office, she drove at an average speed of 90km/hour. On the way home, she drove at an average speed of 60km/hour. How long was her entire roundtrip, in minutes?

   (A) 150
   (B) 90
   (C) 75
   (D) 50

Go on to the next page ➡

10. The students at Sandbanks Elementary School were asked about their favorite sports.

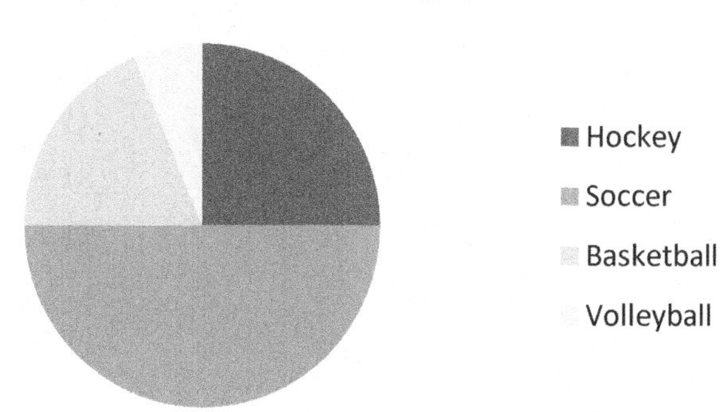

If 91 students picked hockey, approximately how many students are there at the school?

(A) 182
(B) 320
(C) 360
(D) 400

---

11. Julio recorded the heights of several plants in his garden in inches: 2, 3, 5, 7, and 8. What is the product of the average and the range of this list of numbers?

(A) 30
(B) 40
(C) 50
(D) 60

12. A diner offers a lunch combo: customers can choose one of 4 different sandwiches, one of 3 different soups, and either coffee or tea. How many different lunch combinations are possible?

(A) 9
(B) 12
(C) 14
(D) 24

13. David has taken four tests so far in his math class. His scores were 80, 85, 78, and 90. What does David need to get on his fifth test in order to bring his average up to an 86?

(A) 86
(B) 94
(C) 95
(D) 97

14. Which expression is equivalent to the expression $x(x-1)-x+1$?

(A) 0
(B) $(x-1)^2$
(C) x^2-x+1
(D) x^2+1

Go on to the next page ➡

15. The figure below shows a square with side lengths of $\sqrt{2}$ cm that has been inscribed in a circle. What is the area of the shaded region?

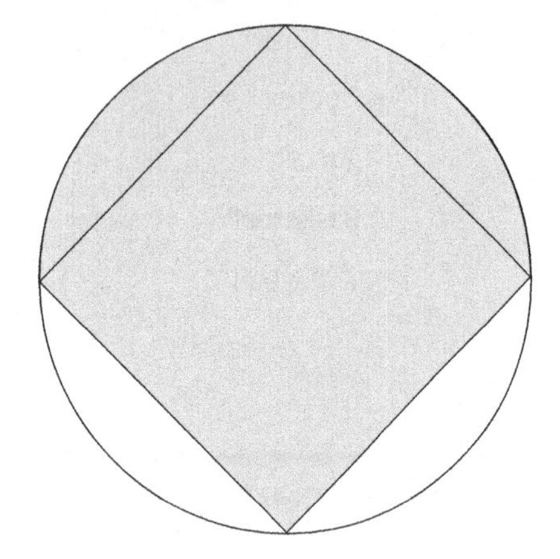

(A) $\frac{\pi}{2} - 2$ cm²

(B) $\pi - 1$ cm²

(C) $\frac{\pi}{2}$ cm²

(D) $\frac{\pi}{2} + 1$ cm²

16. A sequence is shown below. What is the 7th term in this sequence?

$$-\frac{1}{4}, \frac{1}{2}, -1, 2, -4, \ldots$$

(A) -16

(B) 6

(C) 8

(D) 16

17. Use these two functions to answer this question.

$$j(x) = 10x - 3$$
$$k(x) = 3$$

At which point do these two functions intersect?

(A) $(3, 3)$

(B) $\left(3, \frac{6}{10}\right)$

(C) $\left(\frac{3}{5}, 3\right)$

(D) $(10, 3)$

18. The solution set of which inequality is graphed below?

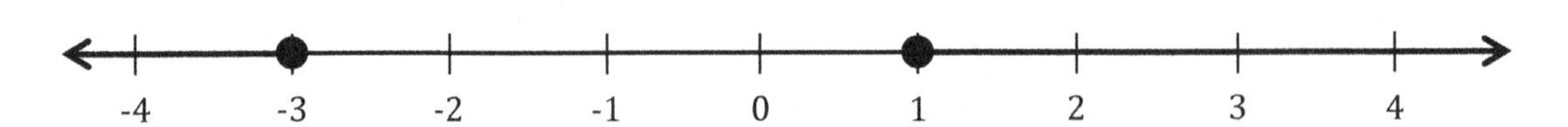

(A) $|x + 1| \geq 2$

(B) $|x - 1| \geq 2$

(C) $|x + 1| > 2$

(D) $|x + 1| \leq 2$

Go on to the next page ➡

19. The stem-and-leaf plot below represents the ages of people at an office.

Stem	Leaf
2	7 8
3	0 2 3 6
4	1 1 5 6 7 8
5	2 3 4 7 9 9
6	1 2 6 9
7	3

5 | 2 represents a 52 year old

What is the median age?

(A) 41
(B) 47
(C) 48
(D) 52

20. The points $(-5, 4)$ and $(7, 12)$ are the endpoints of the diameter of a circle. What are the coordinates of the center of this circle?

(A) $(2, 16)$
(B) $(6, 16)$
(C) $(1, 8)$
(D) $(6, 8)$

21. What is the y-intercept of $y = 3x - 5$?

(A) $\frac{5}{3}$
(B) 3
(C) 5
(D) -5

22. Angles A and B are complementary. If the measure of angle A is 30°, what is the measure of angle B?

(A) 30°
(B) 60°
(C) 90°
(D) 150°

23. If $\frac{1600}{x} = 32$, what is the value of x?

(A) 5
(B) 20
(C) 50
(D) 500

24. Which expression is equivalent to $\sqrt[5]{x^{20}}$?

(A) x^4
(B) x^{10}
(C) x^{15}
(D) x^{25}

25. What is the sum of angles A, B, and C in the diagram below?

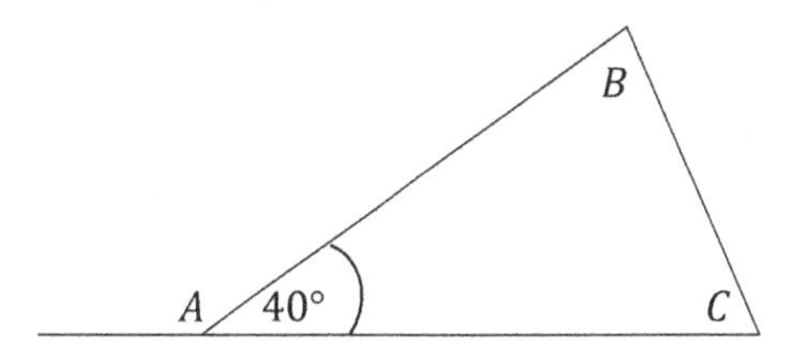

(A) 180°
(B) 280°
(C) 300°
(D) 320°

Go on to the next page ➡

26. If $f(x) = 4x - 3$, what is the value of $f(7)$?

(A) 4
(B) 25
(C) 27
(D) 28

27. What is the product of 243 and 9?

(A) 2185
(B) 2186
(C) 2187
(D) 2188

28. The probability that Meghan scores a goal in soccer is 75%. If she tries 48 times to score a goal, how many times is she expected to miss?

(A) 4
(B) 12
(C) 20
(D) 36

29. Two runners who run at exactly the same speed run laps around a track, shown below.

If the radius of the outer circle is twice the radius of the inner circle, how many laps will the runner on the outside run in the time that it takes the runner on the inside to run 10 laps?

(A) 2.5
(B) 5
(C) 15
(D) 20

30. The table below comes from an equation for a graph.

x	y
-1	0
0	1
1	2
2	9

What is a possible equation for the graph?

(A) $y = x + 1$
(B) $y = x^3$
(C) $y = x^3 + 1$
(D) $y = 3x + 1$

31. The country of Westerovia has an alternate system for money. In this system, 1 coin is equal to 12 papers, 1 paper is equal to 4 beads, and 17 beads are equal to 1 jewel. Which expression represents the number of coins that equals the value of 5 jewels?

(A) $\frac{5}{12\times4\times17}$
(B) $\frac{17}{4\times12}$
(C) $\frac{5\times17}{4\times12}$
(D) $\frac{5\times4\times12}{17}$

32. At 10:00AM, a ship is 50km away from the mainland. If it continues sailing in the same direction away from the mainland at 30km/hour, which expression represents its distance from the mainland (D) in terms of the number of hours past 10:00AM (t)?

(A) $D = 50t + 30$
(B) $D = 10t + 50$
(C) $D = 10t + 30$
(D) $D = 30t + 50$

Go on to the next page ➡

33. What is the solution set for this inequality?

$$-7 < -4x + 1 < 13$$

(A) $-3 < x < -2$

(B) $-3 < x < \frac{3}{2}$

(C) $-3 < x < 2$

(D) $2 < x < 6$

34. Joe and Tyson work on an assembly line at a factory doing quality control. Joe samples $\frac{7}{9}$ of the pens and Tyson samples $\frac{7}{8}$ of the pens. Out of a batch of 72 pens, what is the least number of pens that will be checked by *both* workers?

(A) 16

(B) 47

(C) 56

(D) 63

35. Which is the most reasonable unit to measure the weight of an eraser?

(A) liters

(B) milligrams

(C) grams

(D) kilograms

36. Which numerical expression does NOT represent an integer?

(A) $\frac{\sqrt{12}}{\sqrt{3}}$

(B) $\sqrt{5 + \sqrt{16}}$

(C) $(\sqrt{9})^2 + (\sqrt{2})^2$

(D) $(\sqrt{9} + \sqrt{2})^2$

37. The figure below represents a cake that Luke wants to bake. The formula used to find the volume of a cylinder is $V = r^2 h\pi$, where r is the radius of the cylinder and h is the height of the cylinder.

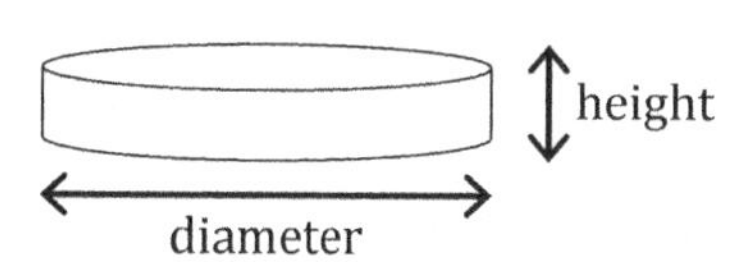

If Luke wants the cake to have a diameter of 10 inches and a height of 3 inches, what will the volume of his cake be?

(A) 45π inches^3

(B) 60π inches^3

(C) 75π inches^3

(D) 90π inches^3

38. Tyler washes the dishes at a rate of fifteen dishes every ten minutes. Harry can only dry the dishes at a rate of fifteen dishes every half hour. If Tyler spends fifty minutes washing the dishes, how long does it take Harry to dry them?

(A) 5 hours and 45 minutes

(B) 3 hours and 20 minutes

(C) 2 hours and 30 minutes

(D) 1 hour and 30 minutes

Go on to the next page ➡

39. Three vertices of a kite are plotted on the graph below.

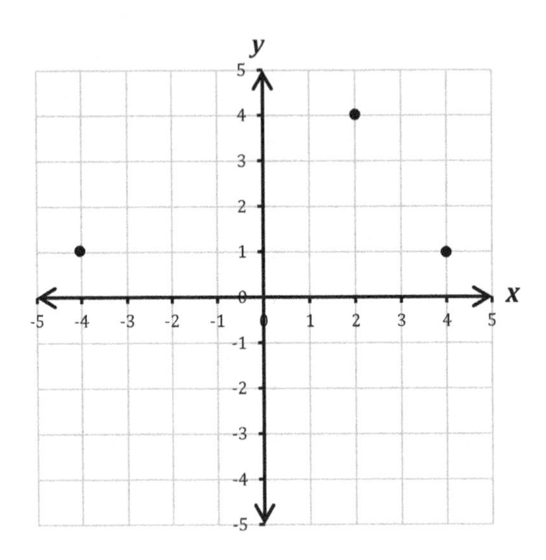

At which point should the fourth vertex be plotted to complete the kite?

(A) $(-2,-2)$

(B) $(-2,4)$

(C) $(-2,2)$

(D) $(2,-2)$

---

40. Corwin used 5 cups of pecans to bake a pie. Each cup of pecans holds about 20 individual nuts. If he is going to split his pie evenly among 8 of his friends, approximately how many pecans will each person get to eat?

(A) 12.5

(B) 10

(C) 2.5

(D) $\frac{5}{8}$

41. The formula for the volume of a cone is $V = \frac{1}{3}\pi r^2 h$, where r is the cone's radius and h is the cone's height.

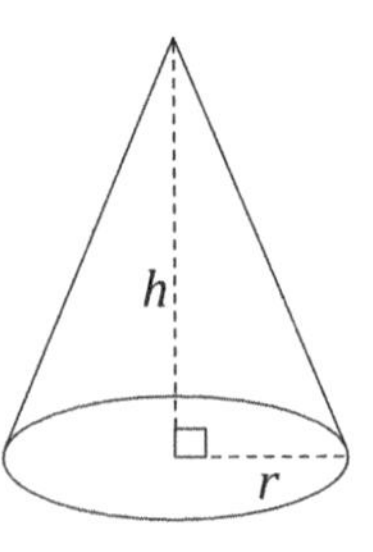

The cone shown above has a height of 5 in. and a radius of $\sqrt{3}$ in. What is the cone's volume?

(A) $\sqrt{3}\pi$ in^2

(B) 3π in^2

(C) 5π in^2

(D) 15π in^2

Go on to the next page ➡

42. If $3(y - 9^m) = 3y - 9$, what is the value of m?

(A) 3

(B) $\sqrt{3}$

(C) $\frac{1}{2}$

(D) 0

43. In the figure below, two congruent regular pentagons have been joined at their bases.

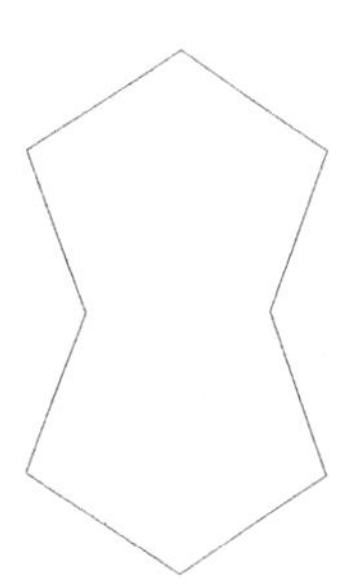

If the perimeter of the entire figure is 40, what is the length of one of the pentagons' sides?

(A) 2

(B) 5

(C) 8

(D) 16

44. The graph below shows the population size and land area of three different towns.

The population density of a town is measured by dividing the town population by the total land size. What is the ratio of the population density of Town A to the population density of Town C?

(A) 3 to 8

(B) 1 to 2

(C) 3 to 4

(D) 4 to 5

Go on to the next page ➡

45. If w is a positive integer, which expression is equivalent to the expression $\sqrt{81x^{4w} - 16y^2}$?

(A) $(3x^w - 4y)(3x^w + 4y)$
(B) $(9x^w - 8y)(9x^w + 8y)$
(C) $(3x^{2w} - 4y^2)(3x^{2w} + 4y^2)$
(D) $(81x^{4w} - 4y^2)(81x^{4w} + 4y^2)$

46. If $A = \begin{bmatrix} 2 & 8 \\ -3 & 7 \end{bmatrix}$ and $B = \begin{bmatrix} 5 & -10 \\ 13 & -11 \end{bmatrix}$, what is $A + B$?

(A) $\begin{bmatrix} 10 & -80 \\ -39 & 77 \end{bmatrix}$

(B) $\begin{bmatrix} 7 & -2 \\ 10 & 4 \end{bmatrix}$

(C) $\begin{bmatrix} -3 & 18 \\ -16 & 4 \end{bmatrix}$

(D) $\begin{bmatrix} 7 & -2 \\ 10 & -4 \end{bmatrix}$

47. Use the triangle below to answer this question.

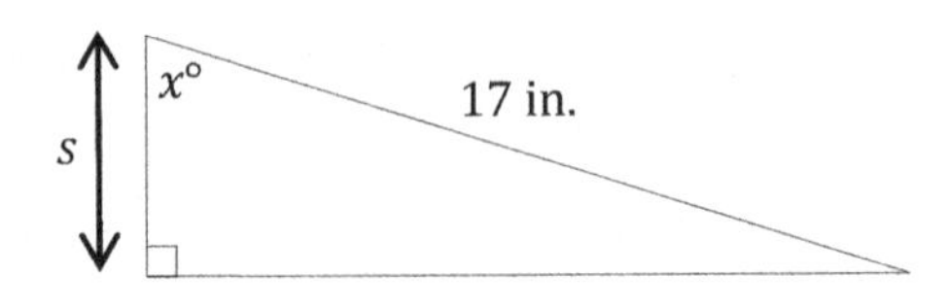

The value of which expression is equal to the length of side s?

(A) $\frac{17\tan(x)}{5}$

(B) $17\sin(x)$

(C) $17\cos(x)$

(D) $\frac{17}{2}\sin(x)$

STOP. Do not go on until told to do so.

STOP

Essay Topic Sheet

The directions for the Essay portion of the ISEE are printed in the box below. Use the pre-lined pages on pages 36-37 for this part of the Practice Test.

You will have 30 minutes to plan and write an essay on the topic printed on the other side of this page. **Do not write on another topic. An essay on another topic is not acceptable.**

The essay is designed to give you an opportunity to show how well you can write. You should try to express your thoughts clearly. How well you write is much more important than how much you write, but you need to say enough for a reader to understand what you mean.

You will probably want to write more than a short paragraph. You should also be aware that a copy of your essay will be sent to each school that will be receiving your test results. You are to write only in the appropriate section of the answer sheet. Please write or print so that your writing may be read by someone who is not familiar with your handwriting.

You may make notes and plan your essay on the reverse side of the page. Allow enough time to copy the final form onto your answer sheet. You must copy the essay topic onto your answer sheet, on page 218, in the box provided.

Please remember to write only the final draft of the essay on pages 36-37 of your answer sheet and to write it in blue or black pen. Again, you may use cursive writing or you may print. Only pages 36-37 will be sent to the schools.

Directions continue on the next page.

REMINDER: Please write this essay topic on the first few lines of the first page of your essay sheet.

Essay Topic

Your local government has a surprising budget surplus, leaving it with extra funds to spend. How do you think the extra funds should be used to improve your community?

- Only write on this essay question
- Only pages 36 and 37 will be sent to the schools
- Only write in blue or black pen

NOTES

PRACTICE TEST 2

UPPER LEVEL

HOW TO TAKE THIS PRACTICE TEST

To simulate an accurate testing environment, sit at a desk in a quiet location free of distractions—no TV, computers, phones, music, or noise—and clear your desk of all materials except pencils and erasers. Remember that no calculators, rulers, protractors, dictionaries, or other aids are allowed on the ISEE.

Give yourself the following amounts of time for each section:

SECTION	SUBJECT	TIME LIMIT
1	Verbal Reasoning	20 minutes
2	Quantitative Reasoning	35 minutes
5 minute break		
3	Reading Comprehension	35 minutes
4	Mathematics Achievement	40 minutes
5 minute break		
5	Essay	30 minutes

Have an adult help you monitor your time, or use a watch and time yourself. Only give yourself the allotted time for each section; put your pencil down when your time is up.

Follow the instructions carefully. As you take your test, bubble your answers into the answer sheets provided. Use the test booklet as scratch paper for notes and calculations. Remember that you are not granted time at the end of a section to transfer your answers to the answer sheet, so you must do this as you go along.

When you are finished, check your answers against the answer keys provided. Then, score your exam using the directions at the end of the book.

Note: students with diagnosed learning disabilities who apply for testing with accommodations may receive extra time, or may be allowed to use certain assistive devices during the ISEE. For more information, visit http://erblearn.org/parents/admission/isee/accommodations.

Ivy Global

ISEE
UPPER LEVEL TEST 2

MARKING INSTRUCTIONS

- Use a #2 or HB pencil only on pages 84 and 85.
- Use a ballpoint pen for your essay on pages 86 and 87.
- Make dark marks that completely fill the circle.
- Erase clearly any mark you wish to change.
- Make no stray marks on this form.
- Do not fold or crease this form.

Correct Mark 

Incorrect Marks 

1 VERBAL REASONING		
1 Ⓐ Ⓑ Ⓒ Ⓓ	15 Ⓐ Ⓑ Ⓒ Ⓓ	29 Ⓐ Ⓑ Ⓒ Ⓓ
2 Ⓐ Ⓑ Ⓒ Ⓓ	16 Ⓐ Ⓑ Ⓒ Ⓓ	30 Ⓐ Ⓑ Ⓒ Ⓓ
3 Ⓐ Ⓑ Ⓒ Ⓓ	17 Ⓐ Ⓑ Ⓒ Ⓓ	31 Ⓐ Ⓑ Ⓒ Ⓓ
4 Ⓐ Ⓑ Ⓒ Ⓓ	18 Ⓐ Ⓑ Ⓒ Ⓓ	32 Ⓐ Ⓑ Ⓒ Ⓓ
5 Ⓐ Ⓑ Ⓒ Ⓓ	19 Ⓐ Ⓑ Ⓒ Ⓓ	33 Ⓐ Ⓑ Ⓒ Ⓓ
6 Ⓐ Ⓑ Ⓒ Ⓓ	20 Ⓐ Ⓑ Ⓒ Ⓓ	34 Ⓐ Ⓑ Ⓒ Ⓓ Lower Level Ends
7 Ⓐ Ⓑ Ⓒ Ⓓ	21 Ⓐ Ⓑ Ⓒ Ⓓ	35 Ⓐ Ⓑ Ⓒ Ⓓ
8 Ⓐ Ⓑ Ⓒ Ⓓ	22 Ⓐ Ⓑ Ⓒ Ⓓ	36 Ⓐ Ⓑ Ⓒ Ⓓ
9 Ⓐ Ⓑ Ⓒ Ⓓ	23 Ⓐ Ⓑ Ⓒ Ⓓ	37 Ⓐ Ⓑ Ⓒ Ⓓ
10 Ⓐ Ⓑ Ⓒ Ⓓ	24 Ⓐ Ⓑ Ⓒ Ⓓ	38 Ⓐ Ⓑ Ⓒ Ⓓ
11 Ⓐ Ⓑ Ⓒ Ⓓ	25 Ⓐ Ⓑ Ⓒ Ⓓ	39 Ⓐ Ⓑ Ⓒ Ⓓ
12 Ⓐ Ⓑ Ⓒ Ⓓ	26 Ⓐ Ⓑ Ⓒ Ⓓ	40 Ⓐ Ⓑ Ⓒ Ⓓ Middle/Upper Level Ends
13 Ⓐ Ⓑ Ⓒ Ⓓ	27 Ⓐ Ⓑ Ⓒ Ⓓ	
14 Ⓐ Ⓑ Ⓒ Ⓓ	28 Ⓐ Ⓑ Ⓒ Ⓓ	

2 QUANTITATIVE REASONING

1 Ⓐ Ⓑ Ⓒ Ⓓ	15 Ⓐ Ⓑ Ⓒ Ⓓ	29 Ⓐ Ⓑ Ⓒ Ⓓ
2 Ⓐ Ⓑ Ⓒ Ⓓ	16 Ⓐ Ⓑ Ⓒ Ⓓ	30 Ⓐ Ⓑ Ⓒ Ⓓ
3 Ⓐ Ⓑ Ⓒ Ⓓ	17 Ⓐ Ⓑ Ⓒ Ⓓ	31 Ⓐ Ⓑ Ⓒ Ⓓ
4 Ⓐ Ⓑ Ⓒ Ⓓ	18 Ⓐ Ⓑ Ⓒ Ⓓ	32 Ⓐ Ⓑ Ⓒ Ⓓ
5 Ⓐ Ⓑ Ⓒ Ⓓ	19 Ⓐ Ⓑ Ⓒ Ⓓ	33 Ⓐ Ⓑ Ⓒ Ⓓ
6 Ⓐ Ⓑ Ⓒ Ⓓ	20 Ⓐ Ⓑ Ⓒ Ⓓ	34 Ⓐ Ⓑ Ⓒ Ⓓ
7 Ⓐ Ⓑ Ⓒ Ⓓ	21 Ⓐ Ⓑ Ⓒ Ⓓ	35 Ⓐ Ⓑ Ⓒ Ⓓ
8 Ⓐ Ⓑ Ⓒ Ⓓ	22 Ⓐ Ⓑ Ⓒ Ⓓ	36 Ⓐ Ⓑ Ⓒ Ⓓ
9 Ⓐ Ⓑ Ⓒ Ⓓ	23 Ⓐ Ⓑ Ⓒ Ⓓ	37 Ⓐ Ⓑ Ⓒ Ⓓ Middle/Upper Level Ends
10 Ⓐ Ⓑ Ⓒ Ⓓ	24 Ⓐ Ⓑ Ⓒ Ⓓ	38 Ⓐ Ⓑ Ⓒ Ⓓ Lower Level Ends
11 Ⓐ Ⓑ Ⓒ Ⓓ	25 Ⓐ Ⓑ Ⓒ Ⓓ	
12 Ⓐ Ⓑ Ⓒ Ⓓ	26 Ⓐ Ⓑ Ⓒ Ⓓ	
13 Ⓐ Ⓑ Ⓒ Ⓓ	27 Ⓐ Ⓑ Ⓒ Ⓓ	
14 Ⓐ Ⓑ Ⓒ Ⓓ	28 Ⓐ Ⓑ Ⓒ Ⓓ	

3 READING COMPREHENSION

1 Ⓐ Ⓑ Ⓒ Ⓓ	15 Ⓐ Ⓑ Ⓒ Ⓓ	29 Ⓐ Ⓑ Ⓒ Ⓓ
2 Ⓐ Ⓑ Ⓒ Ⓓ	16 Ⓐ Ⓑ Ⓒ Ⓓ	30 Ⓐ Ⓑ Ⓒ Ⓓ
3 Ⓐ Ⓑ Ⓒ Ⓓ	17 Ⓐ Ⓑ Ⓒ Ⓓ	31 Ⓐ Ⓑ Ⓒ Ⓓ
4 Ⓐ Ⓑ Ⓒ Ⓓ	18 Ⓐ Ⓑ Ⓒ Ⓓ	32 Ⓐ Ⓑ Ⓒ Ⓓ
5 Ⓐ Ⓑ Ⓒ Ⓓ	19 Ⓐ Ⓑ Ⓒ Ⓓ	33 Ⓐ Ⓑ Ⓒ Ⓓ
6 Ⓐ Ⓑ Ⓒ Ⓓ	20 Ⓐ Ⓑ Ⓒ Ⓓ	34 Ⓐ Ⓑ Ⓒ Ⓓ
7 Ⓐ Ⓑ Ⓒ Ⓓ	21 Ⓐ Ⓑ Ⓒ Ⓓ	35 Ⓐ Ⓑ Ⓒ Ⓓ
8 Ⓐ Ⓑ Ⓒ Ⓓ	22 Ⓐ Ⓑ Ⓒ Ⓓ	36 Ⓐ Ⓑ Ⓒ Ⓓ Middle/Upper Level Ends
9 Ⓐ Ⓑ Ⓒ Ⓓ	23 Ⓐ Ⓑ Ⓒ Ⓓ	
10 Ⓐ Ⓑ Ⓒ Ⓓ	24 Ⓐ Ⓑ Ⓒ Ⓓ	
11 Ⓐ Ⓑ Ⓒ Ⓓ	25 Ⓐ Ⓑ Ⓒ Ⓓ Lower Level Ends	
12 Ⓐ Ⓑ Ⓒ Ⓓ	26 Ⓐ Ⓑ Ⓒ Ⓓ	
13 Ⓐ Ⓑ Ⓒ Ⓓ	27 Ⓐ Ⓑ Ⓒ Ⓓ	
14 Ⓐ Ⓑ Ⓒ Ⓓ	28 Ⓐ Ⓑ Ⓒ Ⓓ	

4 MATHEMATICS ACHIEVEMENT

1 Ⓐ Ⓑ Ⓒ Ⓓ	18 Ⓐ Ⓑ Ⓒ Ⓓ	35 Ⓐ Ⓑ Ⓒ Ⓓ
2 Ⓐ Ⓑ Ⓒ Ⓓ	19 Ⓐ Ⓑ Ⓒ Ⓓ	36 Ⓐ Ⓑ Ⓒ Ⓓ
3 Ⓐ Ⓑ Ⓒ Ⓓ	20 Ⓐ Ⓑ Ⓒ Ⓓ	37 Ⓐ Ⓑ Ⓒ Ⓓ
4 Ⓐ Ⓑ Ⓒ Ⓓ	21 Ⓐ Ⓑ Ⓒ Ⓓ	38 Ⓐ Ⓑ Ⓒ Ⓓ
5 Ⓐ Ⓑ Ⓒ Ⓓ	22 Ⓐ Ⓑ Ⓒ Ⓓ	39 Ⓐ Ⓑ Ⓒ Ⓓ
6 Ⓐ Ⓑ Ⓒ Ⓓ	23 Ⓐ Ⓑ Ⓒ Ⓓ	40 Ⓐ Ⓑ Ⓒ Ⓓ
7 Ⓐ Ⓑ Ⓒ Ⓓ	24 Ⓐ Ⓑ Ⓒ Ⓓ	41 Ⓐ Ⓑ Ⓒ Ⓓ
8 Ⓐ Ⓑ Ⓒ Ⓓ	25 Ⓐ Ⓑ Ⓒ Ⓓ	42 Ⓐ Ⓑ Ⓒ Ⓓ
9 Ⓐ Ⓑ Ⓒ Ⓓ	26 Ⓐ Ⓑ Ⓒ Ⓓ	43 Ⓐ Ⓑ Ⓒ Ⓓ
10 Ⓐ Ⓑ Ⓒ Ⓓ	27 Ⓐ Ⓑ Ⓒ Ⓓ	44 Ⓐ Ⓑ Ⓒ Ⓓ
11 Ⓐ Ⓑ Ⓒ Ⓓ	28 Ⓐ Ⓑ Ⓒ Ⓓ	45 Ⓐ Ⓑ Ⓒ Ⓓ
12 Ⓐ Ⓑ Ⓒ Ⓓ	29 Ⓐ Ⓑ Ⓒ Ⓓ	46 Ⓐ Ⓑ Ⓒ Ⓓ
13 Ⓐ Ⓑ Ⓒ Ⓓ	30 Ⓐ Ⓑ Ⓒ Ⓓ Lower Level Ends	47 Ⓐ Ⓑ Ⓒ Ⓓ Middle/Upper Level Ends
14 Ⓐ Ⓑ Ⓒ Ⓓ	31 Ⓐ Ⓑ Ⓒ Ⓓ	
15 Ⓐ Ⓑ Ⓒ Ⓓ	32 Ⓐ Ⓑ Ⓒ Ⓓ	
16 Ⓐ Ⓑ Ⓒ Ⓓ	33 Ⓐ Ⓑ Ⓒ Ⓓ	
17 Ⓐ Ⓑ Ⓒ Ⓓ	34 Ⓐ Ⓑ Ⓒ Ⓓ	

STUDENT NAME ______________________ GRADE APPLYING FOR ________

Use a blue or black ballpoint pen to write the final draft of your essay on this sheet.

You must write your essay topic in this space.

Use specific details and examples in your response.

Section 1
Verbal Reasoning

40 Questions

Time: 20 minutes

This section is divided into two parts that contain two different types of questions. As soon as you have completed Part One, answer the questions in Part Two. You may write in your test booklet. For each answer you select, fill in the corresponding circle on your answer document.

PART ONE — SYNONYMS

Each question in Part One consists of a word in capital letters followed by four answer choices. Select the one word that is most nearly the same in meaning as the word in capital letters.

SAMPLE QUESTION:

Sample Answer

Ⓐ Ⓑ ● Ⓓ

CHARGE:

(A) release
(B) belittle
(C) accuse
(D) conspire

The correct answer is "accuse," so circle C is darkened.

Go on to the next page ➡

PART TWO — SENTENCE COMPLETION

Each question in Part Two is made up of a sentence with one blank. Each blank indicates that a word or phrase is missing. The sentence is followed by four answer choices. Select the word or phrase that will best complete the meaning of the sentence as a whole.

SAMPLE QUESTIONS: | Sample Answers

It rained so much that the streets were -------. ● Ⓑ Ⓒ Ⓓ

(A) flooded
(B) arid
(C) paved
(D) crowded

The correct answer is "flooded," so circle A is darkened.

The house was so dirty that it took -------. Ⓐ Ⓑ Ⓒ ●

(A) less than ten minutes to wash it.
(B) four months to demolish it.
(C) over a week to walk across it.
(D) two days to clean it.

The correct answer is "two days to clean it," so circle D is darkened.

STOP. Do not go on until told to do so.

PART ONE – SYNONYMS

Directions: Select the word that is most nearly the same in meaning as the word in capital letters.

1. FROLIC
   (A) prance
   (B) jimmy
   (C) laugh
   (D) stride

2. CRUDE
   (A) naked
   (B) insolent
   (C) colorful
   (D) unrefined

3. APPREHEND
   (A) charge
   (B) sentence
   (C) seek
   (D) capture

4. WIRED
   (A) crackling
   (B) captured
   (C) remote
   (D) excited

5. HEEDLESS
   (A) hungry
   (B) inconsiderate
   (C) open
   (D) remorseless

6. ASSIMILATE
   (A) anticipate
   (B) raise
   (C) reject
   (D) incorporate

7. REGIMEN
   (A) army
   (B) king
   (C) plan
   (D) dynasty

8. ASSENT
   (A) justify
   (B) prove
   (C) cultivate
   (D) approve

9. SKULK
   (A) cry
   (B) blossom
   (C) run
   (D) sneak

10. CANTANKEROUS
   (A) grumpy
   (B) uncouth
   (C) immoral
   (D) undeterred

11. TROUNCE
   (A) rout
   (B) denounce
   (C) fish
   (D) captivate

12. MOLTEN
   (A) shed
   (B) pursued
   (C) burnt
   (D) liquefied

Go on to the next page ➡

13. RIGOROUS
    (A) envious
    (B) tactful
    (C) thorough
    (D) cruel

14. CURTAIL
    (A) circle
    (B) rejoice
    (C) limit
    (D) frown

15. AMBITIOUS
    (A) perfect
    (B) bold
    (C) lazy
    (D) careful

16. OVERWHELM
    (A) overpower
    (B) overcook
    (C) overlook
    (D) overthink

17. ADJUST
    (A) judge
    (B) try
    (C) tweak
    (D) carry

18. SQUALL
    (A) snow
    (B) gust
    (C) storm
    (D) thunder

19. BURLY
    (A) belligerent
    (B) muscular
    (C) dour
    (D) angry

Go on to the next page ➡

PART TWO – SENTENCE COMPLETION

Directions: Select the word that best completes the sentence.

20. Amish communities tend to be rather -------, choosing to live in isolated rural areas where they can practice their religion in peace.

    (A) insular
    (B) outgoing
    (C) grave
    (D) fortunate

21. President Abraham Lincoln was known for possessing the virtue of -------; that was how he got the nickname "Honest Abe."

    (A) truthfulness
    (B) malevolence
    (C) caution
    (D) fervor

22. While professional psychics are ------- in their abilities, in experimental settings their predictions are rarely better than random guesses.

    (A) shallow
    (B) confident
    (C) redundant
    (D) noticeable

23. When Watson and Crick discovered the double-helix shape of DNA, it completely changed the ------- of genetic science and opened the door for new genetic research.

    (A) trademarks
    (B) decorations
    (C) fundamentals
    (D) pages

24. While frostbite causes ------- during its onset, affected areas become very painful as they thaw.

    (A) tartness
    (B) dexterity
    (C) numbness
    (D) folly

25. Though I tried to be ------- with my prose, I still went over the word limit for the essay.

    (A) unorthodox
    (B) excessive
    (C) concise
    (D) proper

26. Months of snowstorms and frigid temperatures left many people quite ------- of the weather and ready for spring.

    (A) ignorant
    (B) enamored
    (C) expectant
    (D) weary

27. Canyons are created by the action of rivers ----- their riverbeds over the course of centuries, slowly channeling deep rifts through the earth.

    (A) foraging
    (B) eroding
    (C) regrouping
    (D) replacing

Go on to the next page ➡

28. Journalists prefer to interview ------- people whose answers don't sound forced or rehearsed.
    (A) disheveled
    (B) reluctant
    (C) candid
    (D) meticulous

29. Almost all pastry recipes include a small amount of salt in order to ------- the sweetness of the sugar.
    (A) overwhelm
    (B) counteract
    (C) compound
    (D) taste

30. The ------- of our newly built table proved to be unsound; it collapsed after we put a tablecloth on it.
    (A) intuition
    (B) organization
    (C) abstraction
    (D) construction

31. Garden variety ants are actually capable of ------- feats of strength; worker ants can lift objects many times their own body weight.
    (A) impressive
    (B) nonchalant
    (C) requisite
    (D) complex

32. While bunny slopes are ------ enough for beginning skiers to master, double diamond slopes are ------- for even the most experienced of skiers.
    (A) simple...effortless
    (B) convoluted...unforgiving
    (C) intricate...average
    (D) easy...demanding

33. Working long hours can be financially -------, but ultimately ------ to one's health and social life.
    (A) risky...harmful
    (B) prudent...detrimental
    (C) wise...advantageous
    (D) fortunate...supportive

34. While defense lawyers ------- for their client's interests, the job of the prosecutors is to ------ the state's case against them.
    (A) obfuscate...prove
    (B) support...predict
    (C) advocate...argue
    (D) provoke...restrict

35. In fairy tales, knights are often models of ------- who exhibit all virtues and never commit ------- deeds.
    (A) excellence...altruistic
    (B) chivalry...malicious
    (C) opulence...sinister
    (D) rebellion...arrogant

36. While children are often ------- by the tricks of magicians, adults usually find them too ------- to be entertaining.
    (A) enraged...simplistic
    (B) overjoyed...perplexing
    (C) fascinated...transparent
    (D) amused...realistic

37. Large cities produce such ------- amounts of garbage that finding landfills ------- enough to hold all the refuse can be difficult.
    (A) copious...sizeable
    (B) colossal...fallacious
    (C) frequent...adequate
    (D) fearful...comical

Go on to the next page ➡

38. Cooking good risotto requires much ------- on the part of the chef; cook the risotto too quickly, and it will clump together and become -------.

    (A) patience...inedible
    (B) aptitude...appetizing
    (C) frustration...unsalvageable
    (D) preparation...mysterious

39. The Soviet Union invested ------- in the Kola Superdeep Borehole, yet still ultimately failed to ------- their target depth of 15,000 meter.

    (A) endlessly...relieve
    (B) tremendously...achieve
    (C) intermittently...possess
    (D) retroactively...accomplish

40. Though eating junk food is often ------- in the moment, it can make you feel ------- and bloated afterward.

    (A) sickening...refreshed
    (B) gratifying...disorganized
    (C) fattening...fabulous
    (D) satisfying...uncomfortable

STOP. Do not go on until told to do so.

Section 2
Quantitative Reasoning

38 Questions | **Time: 35 minutes**

Each question is followed by four suggested answers. Read each question and then decide which one of the four suggested answers is best.

Find the row of spaces on your answer document that has the same number as the question. In this row, mark the space having the same letter as the answer you have chosen. You may write in your test booklet.

SAMPLE QUESTIONS:

Sample Answers

What is the value of the expression $(4 + 6) \div 2$?

Ⓐ Ⓑ ● Ⓓ

(A) 2
(B) 4
(C) 5
(D) 7

The correct answer is 5, so circle C is darkened.

A square has an area of $25cm^2$. What is the length of one of its sides?

Ⓐ ● Ⓒ Ⓓ

(A) 1 cm
(B) 5 cm
(C) 10 cm
(D) 25 cm

The correct answer is 5, so circle B is darkened.

Go on to the next page ➡

PART TWO — QUANTITATIVE COMPARISONS

All questions in Part Two are quantitative comparisons between the quantities shown in Column A and Column B. Using the information given in each question, compare the quantity in Column A to the quantity in Column B, and choose one of these four answer choices:

(A) The quantity in Column A is greater.

(B) The quantity in Column B is greater.

(C) The two quantities are equal.

(D) The relationship cannot be determined from the information given.

SAMPLE QUESTIONS:

Column A	Column B	Sample Answer
5	$\sqrt{25}$	Ⓐ Ⓑ ● Ⓓ

The quantity in Column A (5) is the same as the quantity in Column B (5), so circle C is darkened.

$x = 6^2 - 3 \times 4$

Column A	Column B	Sample Answer
x	22	● Ⓑ Ⓒ Ⓓ

The quantity in Column A (24) is greater than the quantity in Column B (22), so circle A is darkened.

STOP. Do not go on until told to do so.

STOP

PART ONE – WORD PROBLEMS

Directions: Choose the best answer from the four choices given.

1. If $5 \geq x > -3$, what is the minimum value for y if $y = x^2 - 9$?

   (A) -9
   (B) -3
   (C) 0
   (D) 3

2. Jerry has b car brand names available. Once a brand name is selected, it cannot be selected again. If Jerry selects two cars at random, what is the probability that one of his choices will be a Cool Look brand name car?

   (A) $\frac{2}{b}$
   (B) $\frac{b-2}{b}$
   (C) $\frac{1}{b^2}$
   (D) $2b$

3. A train is moving at 55 miles per hour. A car is moving in the exact opposite direction at s miles per hour. After 2 hours what will be the distance between the train and the car?

   (A) $55 + 2s$ miles
   (B) $2(55 + s)$ miles
   (C) $2s$ miles
   (D) $2(55 - s)$ miles

4. g⬀ $= \left(\frac{5}{g}\right)^2 - 4^g$. What is the value of $\frac{1}{x}$⬀ ?

   (A) $\frac{1}{\left(\frac{5}{x}\right)^2 - 4^x}$
   (B) $(5x)^2 - 2$
   (C) $(5x)^2 - \sqrt[x]{4}$
   (D) $(5x)^2 - \frac{1}{4^x}$

5. A company wants to use sixty-four trucks to bring goods from its warehouses to its headquarters. All the warehouses are located along one highway. Each warehouse loads three quarters of the trucks that arrive or loads one truck, whichever is greater. A truck that has been loaded returns to headquarters, while the remaining empty trucks drive to the next warehouse. How many warehouses will the fleet of sixty-four trucks visit before every truck has returned to headquarters?

   (A) 1
   (B) 2
   (C) 3
   (D) 4

6. What is the value of the expression $\frac{8^{(2/3)} + 4^{(3/2)}}{2^3}$?

   (A) $\frac{17}{16}$
   (B) $\frac{3}{2}$
   (C) $\frac{\sqrt[3]{4}}{2\sqrt{2}}$
   (D) $\frac{1280}{3}$

7. The product of all integers from -1 to -100, inclusive is z. What is the product of all integers from -2 to -102 inclusive?

   (A) $-z$
   (B) $\frac{-z \times 10302}{2}$
   (C) $-z \times 10302$
   (D) $z \times 10302$

Go on to the next page ➡

8. If $2y - x = 6$, then which expression is equal to x?

   (A) $-2(3 + y)$
   (B) $-2(3 - y)$
   (C) $2(3 - y)$
   (D) $2(3 + y)$

9. Helen ran an average of 15 miles per day for 5 days. After six days of running, her mean distance was 12.5 miles. How many miles did Helen run on the sixth day?

   (A) 0
   (B) 2.5
   (C) 12.5
   (D) 15

10. A trapezoid has two bases. One of the bases measures 5 inches and the other measures 7 inches. If its total area is 36 inches^2, what is the measure of its height?

    (A) 6 inches
    (B) 12 inches
    (C) 35 inches
    (D) 36 inches

11. A general manager is trying to figure out the cost of making a fruit drink. She knows that the cost of berries and bananas together are equal to the cost of the drink and that a fruit drink with only bananas is $1 less expensive than one with both bananas and berries. What other information does she need in order to complete her calculation of the cost of the fruit drink?

    (A) the cost of electricity used to make the fruit drink
    (B) the comparable cost of pomegranates
    (C) that berries are selling for one half the cost of a banana
    (D) that berries are the most desired fruit for customers

12. A right angle triangle's hypotenuse increases 25 percent from 20cm. If the triangle's new base is 20cm, what is the new triangle's area?

    (A) 96cm^2
    (B) 150cm^2
    (C) 300cm^2
    (D) 500cm^2

13. An equilateral triangle is inscribed within a circle.

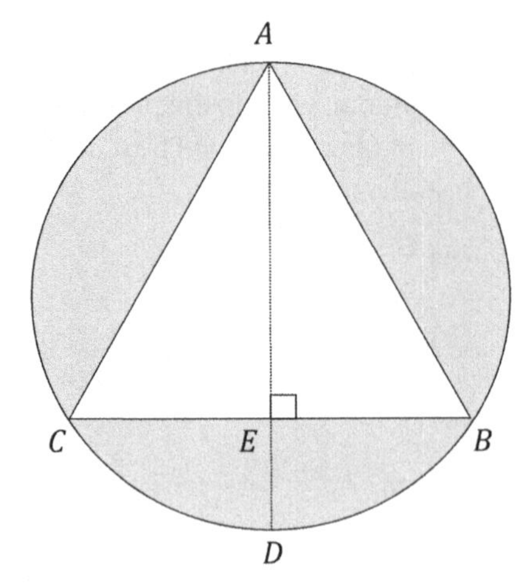

If $\overline{AD} = 2$, $\overline{AE} = \frac{3}{2}$, and $\overline{CB} = \sqrt{3}$, what is area of the entire shaded region?

(A) $\frac{3\sqrt{3}}{4}$
(B) $\pi - \frac{3\sqrt{3}}{4}$
(C) $4\pi - 3\sqrt{3}$
(D) 2π

Go on to the next page ➡

14. The number of days of sunshine per month in Toronto are represented on a histogram.

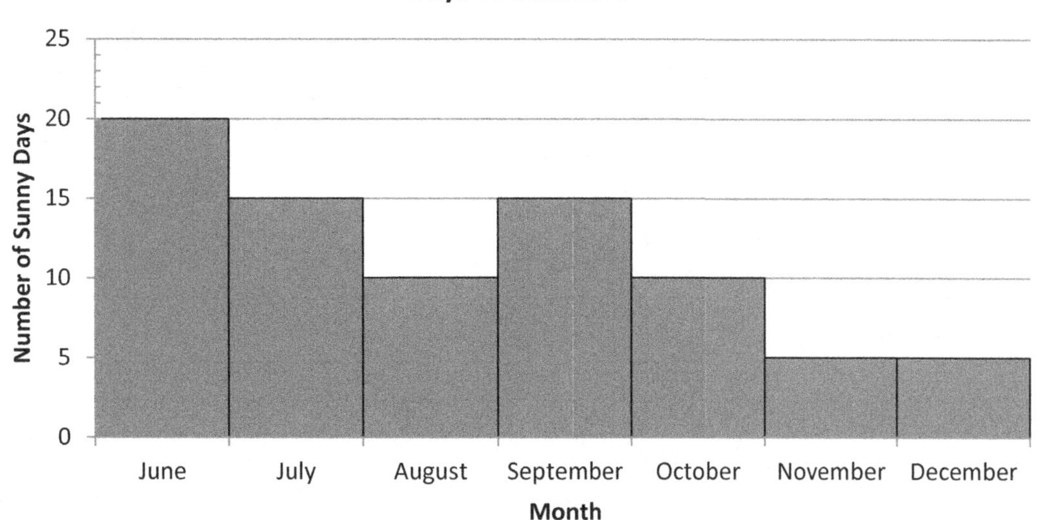

Which of the following statements is correct?

(A) On average from June to December, Toronto is sunny more often than not.

(B) The graph has a single mode of 5 sunny days.

(C) The median number of sunny days is equal to the number of sunny days in August.

(D) The average number of sunny days per month is greater than the range of sunny days per month.

---

15. A is the least common multiple of 12 and 18. B is the smallest prime factor of 12 and 18. What is A/B?

(A) $\frac{1}{6}$

(B) 6

(C) 12

(D) 18

16. What is the value of the expression $\frac{\sqrt[3]{3^4}}{\sqrt[6]{3^{-2}}}$?

(A) 1

(B) $\sqrt[3]{3}$

(C) 3

(D) $3\sqrt[3]{3^2}$

Go on to the next page ➡

17. If x is a negative integer and $x^2 - 9 = 0$, what is the value of x?

    (A) -9

    (B) -6

    (C) -3

    (D) -1

18. A sphere is placed inside a pyramid as shown below. The pyramid's base is 12 and its height is $\sqrt{6}$. The formula used to find the volume of a pyramid is $V = \frac{base \times height}{3}$.

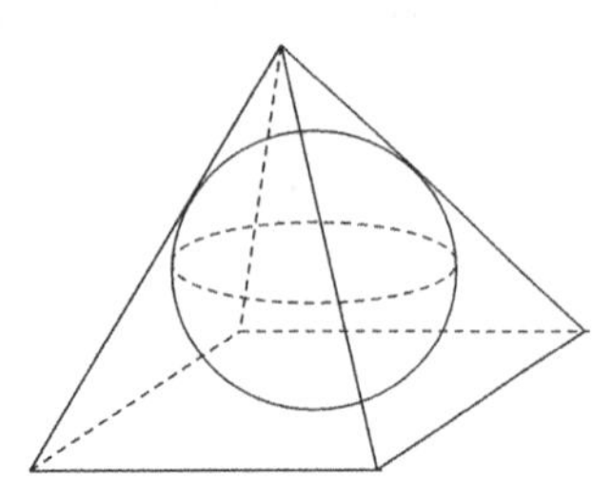

If the volume of the sphere is $\frac{4\pi}{3}$, what is the volume of the empty space left inside the pyramid?

    (A) $2\sqrt{3} - \frac{4}{3}\pi$

    (B) $4\sqrt{6} - \frac{4}{3}\pi$

    (C) $8\sqrt{3} - \frac{4}{3}\pi$

    (D) $8\sqrt{6} - \frac{4}{3}\pi$

19. An isosceles triangle is shown.

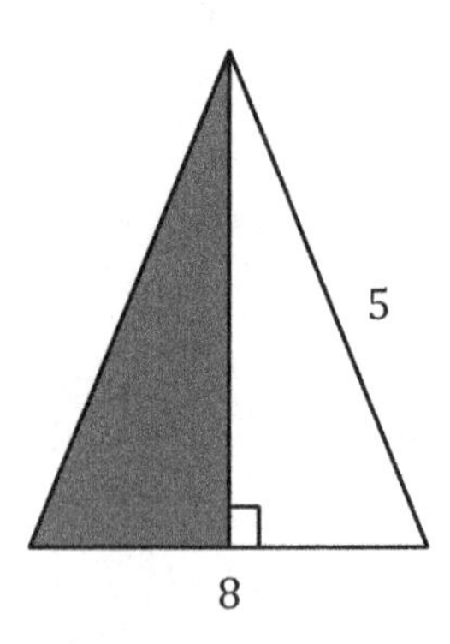

Note: Figure not drawn to scale.

The triangle has a base of 8, a side of 5, and is bisected through the middle. What is the perimeter of the shaded region?

    (A) 12

    (B) 14

    (C) 18

    (D) 24

Go on to the next page ➡

20. The time for 10 competitors at an eating competition is shown on a graph. The competitors each eat one at a time and their times are recorded.

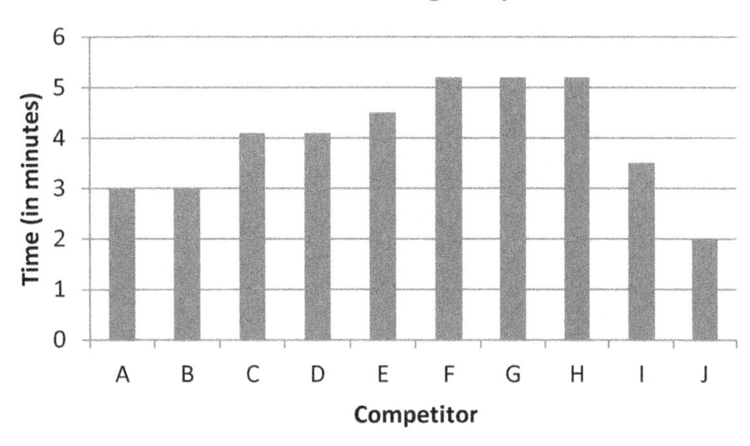

Which of the following statements is true?

(A) The range for the competitors' times is greater than the competitors' mean time.

(B) The competition lasted approximately 35 minutes.

(C) The mode time for the competitors is less than the competitors' mean time.

(D) The range of the competitors' times is less than the competitors' mean time.

Go on to the next page ➡

PART TWO – QUANTITATIVE COMPARISONS

Directions: Using the information given in each question, compare the quantity in column A to the quantity in Column B. All questions in Part Two have these answer choices:

(A) The quantity in Column A is greater.

(B) The quantity in Column B is greater.

(C) The two quantities are equal.

(D) The relationship cannot be determined from the information given.

$\&j = 2(2^j - 6)$

	Column A	Column B
21.	&3	6

	Column A	Column B
22.	$\sqrt[3]{3^{-3}}$	$\frac{1}{2}$

	Column A	Column B
23.	$3 \times -2 + \left(\frac{3}{2} - 4\right) \times 2$	-12

	Column A	Column B
24.	$-\frac{1}{3}$	The slope of the line perpendicular to the expression $2x + 5 - y = 0$

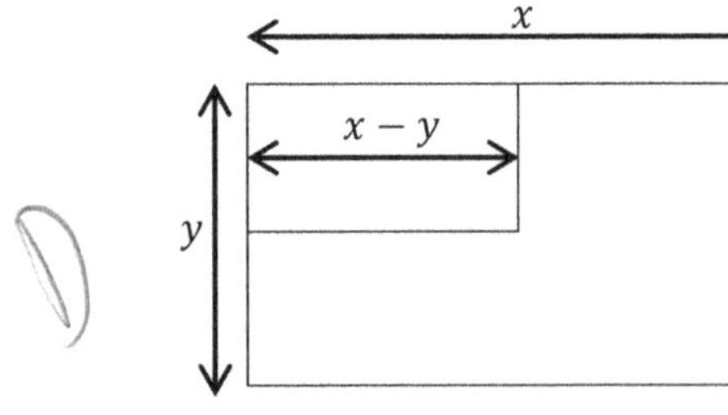

Note: Figure not drawn to scale.

	Column A	Column B
25.	$2y^2$	The area of the rectangle

An 8 sided number octahedron, labelled 1-8, is rolled twice.

	Column A	Column B
26.	The probability that the sum of the rolls will equal eight	$\frac{1}{8}$

There are two types of house, Modern and Classic, and each house may be painted red, yellow, green, blue, grey, or white.

	Column A	Column B
27.	The probability that James will pick a Modern type of house with a blue color	The probability that James will pick a Classic house with a color other than yellow

---

	Column A	Column B
28.	The area of a circle with a radius of b.	The area of a square with a side of $2b$.

Go on to the next page ➡

ANSWER CHOICES FOR ALL QUESTIONS ON THIS PAGE:

(A) The quantity in Column A is greater.
(B) The quantity in Column B is greater.
(C) The two quantities are equal.
(D) The relationship cannot be determined from the information given.

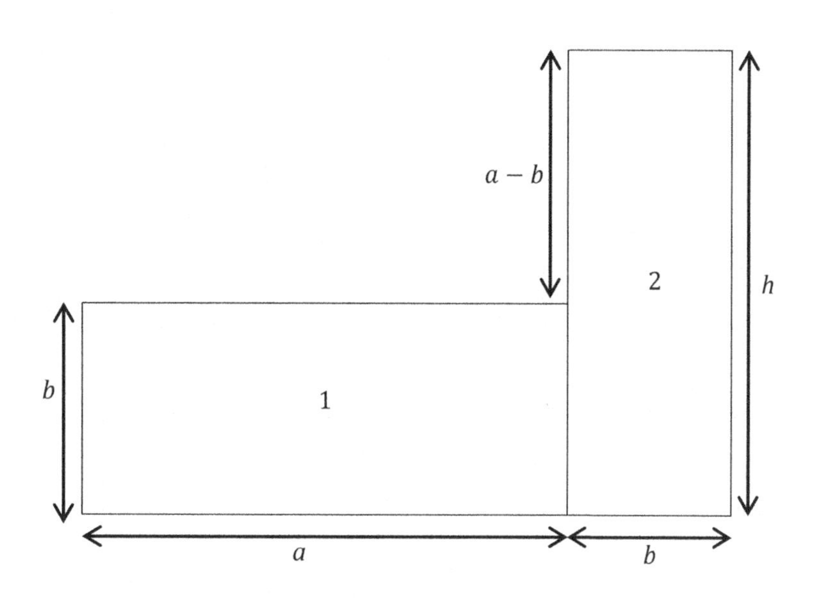

Note: Figures not drawn to scale.

	Column A	Column B
29.	The area of rectangle *2* if $h = 2b$	The area of rectangle *1* if $h = 2b$

A box-and-whisker graph represents the difference of high to low tide in 19 locations by the sea.

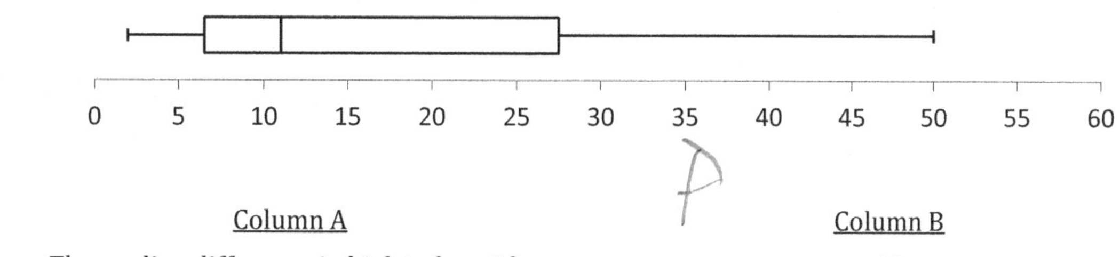

	Column A	Column B
30.	The median difference in high to low tide	10

Go on to the next page ➡

ANSWER CHOICES FOR ALL QUESTIONS ON THIS PAGE:

(A) The quantity in Column A is greater.
(B) The quantity in Column B is greater.
(C) The two quantities are equal.
(D) The relationship cannot be determined from the information given.

	Column A	Column B
31.	$2 + \frac{2p+4}{3}$	$\frac{2p}{3} + 4$

Gum costs \$2.80 and is paid for by Eduardo using nickels and dimes. Eduardo paid with 3 times as many dimes as nickels.

One nickel=\$0.05, one dime=\$0.10

	Column A	Column B
32.	The number of nickels that Eduardo uses	8

In January, 2014 the cost of crude oil was approximately \$108 dollar per barrel. By the end of February, 2014 the price increased by 20%. By the end of March, 2014 the price decreased by 20%.

	Column A	Column B
33.	The price of a barrel of oil at the end of March, 2014	\$108

$$a = 2 \times \left(3 - 5\left(\frac{8}{2^2} - 1\right) + \frac{3^2}{2}\right) - 2$$

	Column A	Column B
34.	25% *of a*	$3/b$

The area of rectangle C is three times the area of rectangle B.

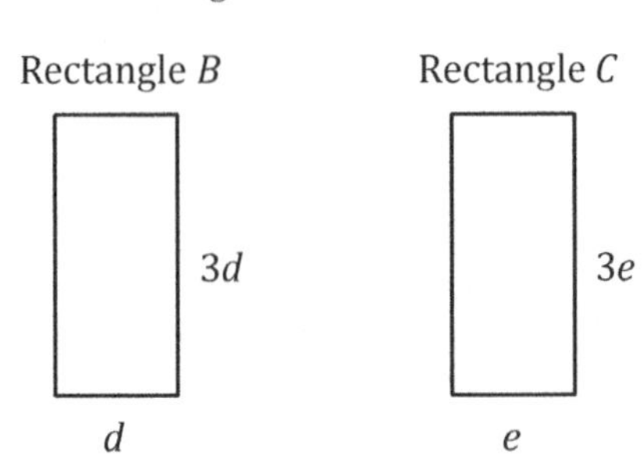

Note: Figures not drawn to scale.

	Column A	Column B
35.	The perimeter of rectangle B	$\frac{8e}{\sqrt{3}}$

Jill rolls a 2 on a 6 sided cube, numbered 1-6. She then rolls the 6 cube two more times.

	Column A	Column B
36.	The probability that she rolls two more 2s	$\frac{1}{36}$

A jar is filled with nickels and dimes and the sum of the money in the jar = s. There are three times more dimes than nickels in the jar. (One nickel = \$0.05 and one dime = \$0.10.)

	Column A	Column B
37.	The number of nickels in the jar	$\frac{s}{0.30}$

STOP. Do not go on until told to do so.

Section 3
Reading Comprehension

36 Questions | **Time: 35 minutes**

This section contains six short reading passages. Each passage is followed by six questions based on its content. Answer the questions following each passage on the basis of what is stated or implied in that passage. You may write in your test booklet.

STOP. Do not go on until told to do so.

Questions 1–6

1 According to a press release from the University of Buffalo, university researchers are developing an underwater wireless network that they are dubbing a "deep-sea" Internet. If this network proves successful, it could lead to improvements in tsunami detection, offshore oil and natural gas exploration, surveillance, pollution monitoring and other marine activities.

10 "A submerged wireless network will give us an unprecedented ability to collect and analyze data from our oceans in real time," said Tommaso Melodia, an associate professor of electrical engineering and the project's lead researcher. "Making this information available to anyone with a smartphone or computer, especially when a tsunami or other type of disaster occurs, could help save lives."

19 The need for a submerged wireless network arises from the limitations of land-based wireless networks. These networks rely on radio waves that transmit data via satellites and antennae. While very effective at transmitting information over land, radio waves work poorly underwater. In order to communicate underwater, organizations like the Navy and National Oceanic and Atmospheric Administration must use sound wave-based techniques instead. For example, NOAA relies on acoustic waves to send data from tsunami sensors on the seafloor to surface buoys. The buoys then convert the acoustic waves into radio waves to send the data to a satellite, which then redirects the radio waves back to land-based computers. This can be a cumbersome process because each system has a different infrastructure specific to the type of waves it can receive, and data must be converted from one system to the next.

40 Melodia's new framework builds upon existing sound-wave based technology to eliminate many of these tedious steps. Instead of shuttling data back and forth among different sensors, it would transmit data from existing underwater sensor networks to laptops, smartphones and other wireless devices in real time.

48 The system was recently tested in Lake Erie. Melodia and his fellow researchers lowered two 40-pound sensors into the water, typed a command into a laptop, and seconds later a series of high-pitched chirps ricocheted off a nearby concrete wall. These chirps acted as an aural confirmation of the network's success.

56 Melodia believes that the implications of such technology are many. "We could even use it to monitor fish and marine mammals, and find out how to best protect them from shipping traffic and other dangers," Melodia explained. "An Internet underwater has so many possibilities."

Go on to the next page ➡

1. The primary purpose of the passage is to
   (A) explain the structure of the Internet and contrast it with its marine counterpart.
   (B) discredit Tommaso Melodia's ideas.
   (C) discuss the potential impact of a developing marine technology.
   (D) promote doing electronic activities underwater.

2. In line 36, the word "cumbersome" most nearly means
   (A) inefficient
   (B) heavy
   (C) streamlined
   (D) erratic

3. According to the third paragraph (lines 19-39), one reason that the current system of underwater sound wave technology works poorly is that
   (A) data must be converted numerous times between different systems.
   (B) buoys can only absorb acoustic waves.
   (C) the Navy and NOAA don't understand it very well.
   (D) we have no underwater satellites.

4. The first quote from Tommaso Melodia (lines 10-12) implies that
   (A) a submerged wireless network would replace the Internet over time.
   (B) we have previously been unable to process underwater data in real time.
   (C) there are not enough data analysts to process all of the underwater data.
   (D) this submerged wireless network is replacing an older one.

5. The experiment conducted in Lake Erie (lines 49-55) demonstrated that
   (A) the new framework could be disruptive to fish, marine mammals, and shipping traffic.
   (B) this new technology only works in bodies of freshwater.
   (C) commands from land-based wireless devices could be successfully converted into acoustic waves.
   (D) the submerged wireless network is not yet operational.

6. The final quote from Tommaso Melodia (lines 57-60) implies that
   (A) "underwater Internet" has only a limited range of possible effects.
   (B) protecting marine mammals is the entire goal of the submerged wireless network.
   (C) saving marine life is one possible benefit of the submerged wireless network.
   (D) a submerged wireless network would be bad for the shipping industry.

Go on to the next page ➡

Questions 7–12

1 People have always been attracted to
2 water. Many of the great civilizations of the
3 past originated near seas, lakes, and rivers.
4 There are many good reasons to live near
5 bodies of water. Rivers flowing to the sea
6 provide fresh water for people, livestock, and
7 crops. Floodplains and sediments enrich the
8 soil, making farming easier and crops more
9 abundant. Even the salty seas provide access to
10 plentiful fisheries, supplying ample food for the
11 human population, as well as access to
12 navigable waterways that make large scale
13 commerce possible by allowing people to load
14 goods onto boats for transportation over long
15 distances.
16 By some estimates, more than half of the
17 planet's current population lives in coastal
18 regions, and the population of coastal regions is
19 growing more rapidly than the non-coastal
20 population. Living near the coast is a mixed
21 blessing, however. The sea still offers access to
22 shipping lanes, fisheries, and other natural
23 resources, but coastal waters are becoming
24 increasingly polluted. Sewage discharge in
25 densely populated areas is a major contributor
26 to marine pollution and is responsible for the
27 spread of infection and disease. Pesticides from
28 farms, and industrial pollutants from factories,
29 power plants, and other sources also find their
30 way into the sea from inland farms and
31 factories and can taint fish stocks, shellfish, and
32 even seaweed, making food harvested from the
33 sea potentially unsafe for human consumption.
34 Additionally, as the planet warms and sea
35 levels rise, coastal areas are under increasing
36 threat from storm surges, or, in some cases, in
37 danger of being entirely submerged by rising
38 waters. Millions of people could be displaced
39 by rising seas in the century to come and
40 billions of dollars' worth of real estate washed
41 away by the mounting waters.
42 But disaster is not inevitable:
43 governments, non-profit organizations, and
44 major corporations are all exploring ways of
45 confronting the challenges faced by coastal
46 regions. Plans are being drawn and projects are
47 underway to help clean up polluted coastal
48 regions and prepare for the dangers of a
49 climatically changing world. Some of the
50 measures being considered, such as high
51 seawalls designed to protect cities from rising
52 waters, are massive and incredibly expensive
53 projects. But even with increasing
54 environmental threats, the human population
55 is unlikely to abandon the coasts any time soon,
56 and such investments may be necessary to
57 secure our future by the sea.

Go on to the next page ➡

7. The tone of the second paragraph could best be described as
   (A) indecisive.
   (B) ambitious.
   (C) bleak.
   (D) pithy.

8. What is the main purpose of the first paragraph?
   (A) to persuade readers to move to the coast
   (B) to describe the ancient civilizations that arose along coasts
   (C) to discuss the benefits of living near water
   (D) to foreshadow changes that would later happen in coastal areas

9. In line 31, the word "taint" most nearly means
   (A) improve
   (B) massacre
   (C) corrupt
   (D) contaminate

10. In the second paragraph (lines 16-41), the author cites all of the following coastal pollution sources EXCEPT
    (A) fuel runoff from shipping boats.
    (B) sewage discharge from highly populated areas.
    (C) pesticides from agricultural activities.
    (D) pollutants from power plants.

11. The final paragraph (lines 42-57) implies that
    (A) the measures necessary to combat coastal pollution are too expensive to enact.
    (B) human beings will do whatever is necessary to continue living in coastal areas.
    (C) it is too late to effect serious change in coastal regions.
    (D) only sea-based industries are interested in stemming coastal pollution.

12. The primary message of this passage is that
    (A) without expensive sea walls, coastal cities may be more vulnerable to flooding in the future.
    (B) pollution and climate change pose growing threats to coastal populations.
    (C) coastal regions will inevitably disappear.
    (D) the sea was more useful to ancient human populations than current ones.

Go on to the next page ➡

RC

Questions 13–18

1 Henri Marie Raymond de Toulouse-
2 Lautrec-Monfa—or more simply, Henri de
3 Toulouse-Lautrec—was a French painter and
4 illustrator whose immersion in the colorful life
5 of Paris in the last decades of the 19th century
6 yielded a collection of exciting, elegant, and
7 provocative images. Henri owed his long name
8 to his aristocratic heritage, to which he also
9 owed his serious life-long health problems.
10 Henri's parents, the Count and Countess of
11 Toulouse and Lautrec, were first cousins, and
12 Henri suffered from health conditions often
13 found in the offspring of close relatives. At the
14 age of 13, Henri fractured his right thigh bone,
15 and at 14, his left. The breaks did not heal
16 properly, and his legs ceased to grow, so that as
17 an adult he was just over five feet tall, having
18 developed an adult-sized torso while retaining
19 his child-sized legs. Physically unable to
20 participate in many activities typically enjoyed
21 by men of his age, Henri immersed himself in
22 art.
23 Under the tutelage of Bonnat and later
24 Fernand Cormon, Henri developed his
25 characteristically vivid painting style and his
26 taste for the Paris social scene as his main
27 artistic subject. He was masterful at capturing
28 crowd scenes in which all of the figures are
29 highly individualized; the evocative images
30 buzz with life, bringing the observer into the
31 humming and colorful social events of Paris.
32 Along with Cézanne, Van Gogh, and Gauguin,
33 Henri Toulouse-Lautrec would come to be
34 known as one of the greatest painters of the
35 period.
36 Sadly, as with many great artists, Henri's
37 life was cut short by tragedy. Constantly
38 mocked for his short stature and physical
39 appearance, Henri drowned his sorrows in
40 alcohol. His alcoholism eventually became so
41 debilitating that his mother briefly had him
42 institutionalized. Despite her and the rest of his
43 family's best efforts, Henri died from
44 complications due to alcoholism at the young
45 age of 36. One wonders what Henri's art career
46 would have been like if he had lived to old age.

Go on to the next page ➡

13. Based on the description in the passage, the paintings of Henri de Toulouse-Lautrec are most likely
    (A) drab.
    (B) abstract.
    (C) satirical.
    (D) vibrant.

14. The author states that Henri's long name and physical ailments were both a result of
    (A) malnutrition as a child.
    (B) his talent as a painter.
    (C) his lack of athletic ability.
    (D) his aristocratic origins.

15. According to the author's description in the second paragraph (lines 23-35), Henri's masterpieces
    (A) were inspired by his engagement in the social life of his city.
    (B) were successful due to his family's influence.
    (C) cured him of his disabilities.
    (D) allowed him to keep living the life of an aristocrat.

16. According to the passage, Henri's stunted growth
    (A) raised his social status.
    (B) prevented him from enjoying certain experiences with his peers.
    (C) directly caused his death.
    (D) was common among artists in Paris during this period.

17. Which of the following does the author consider one of Henri's greatest strengths as a painter?
    (A) His inspiring biography.
    (B) His ability to spark controversy with his illustrations.
    (C) His memorable appearance.
    (D) His ability to portray individual people within a large crowd.

18. Based on the information in the passage, Fernand Cormon was most likely
    (A) one of Henri's childhood friends.
    (B) one of Henri's relatives.
    (C) one of Henri's art teachers.
    (D) Henri's patron in London.

Go on to the next page ➡

Questions 19–24

In a settlement called Pormpuraaw, on the northern tip of the Cape York Peninsula in Queensland, Australia, live a people called the Thaayorre. The Thaayorre speak a language called Kuuk Thaayorre, which shares several important features with other aboriginal languages: it is spoken by only a few hundred people (two hundred and fifty, at the last count); most of the dialects have been lost as the number of speakers has dwindled; and, in Kuuk Thaayorre, there is no word for "left" or "right." In fact, in Kuuk Thaayorre there is no subjective direction at all. All sixteen words for direction relate to the cardinal directions: North, East, South and West.

Kuuk Thaayorre uses cardinal directions instead of subjective direction at all scales, large and small. If you were speaking Kuuk Thaayorre, not only might you have to say something familiar like "you must walk north to reach the store," but you might also have to say something like "your southeastern shoe is untied." If you lost track of your position relative to the cardinal directions, then you wouldn't be able to communicate effectively at all.

Owing to this peculiarity of their language, the Thaayorre people must always know which direction they are facing, even when they are inside or in unfamiliar surroundings. Fortunately, as recent research demonstrates, the Thaayorre and other people who speak similar languages have a special talent for this. They're even better at tracking their orientation than scientists had previously thought was possible among human beings.

This absolute dependence on cardinal directions may affect other areas of the Thaayorre people's lives as well. For example, when asked to arrange a sequence of pictures in temporal order, Kuuk Thaayorre speakers consistently arrange them so that time runs east to west, regardless of their own bodily orientation. Speakers of English, however, generally arrange them so that time runs from left to right from the perspective of the person arranging the pictures. Researchers are intrigued by this difference in the visualization of time, and have speculated about the possibility of broader differences.

The Thaayorre's abilities and peculiarities raise questions about the power of the human mind to achieve what was once thought impossible, and about the relationship between language and thought processes.

Go on to the next page ➡

19. What does the author mean by "subjective direction" (line 17)?
    (A) Directions which are always the opposite of objective directions.
    (B) Directions unique to aboriginal languages.
    (C) Directions that rely on descriptions of landmarks.
    (D) Directions that are unrelated to the cardinal directions.

20. The author would most likely agree with which of the following statements about the Thaayorre people?
    (A) They cannot communicate effectively.
    (B) They think more clearly about things than most other people.
    (C) Their culture will soon be extinct.
    (D) Their language and abilities raise questions about human potential.

21. The author implies that English speakers, unlike the Kuuk Thayyorre, normally use cardinal directions only
    (A) on large scales, for things that are big or far away.
    (B) when they are inside.
    (C) on small scales, for things that are small or nearby.
    (D) when they cannot tell which way they are facing.

22. We can infer from the passage that
    (A) other aboriginal languages also rely heavily on cardinal directions.
    (B) scientists don't understand how we track subjective directions.
    (C) cardinal directions are better than subjective directions.
    (D) English has no words for cardinal directions.

23. What is the structure of this passage?
    (A) Two differing opinions are given about a popular issue, but evidence is provided for only one side.
    (B) A specific phenomenon is discussed, along with speculation about its implications.
    (C) One author discredits the ideas of another author.
    (D) A complicated but important concept is explained in detail.

24. In line 37, the word "absolute" most nearly means
    (A) sole.
    (B) radical.
    (C) ineffective.
    (D) ludicrous.

Go on to the next page ➡

Questions 25–30

1 Charlotte, Emily, and Anne Bronte were
2 born in the early 19th century to Patrick, a
3 priest, and Maria Bronte. The sisters had two
4 elder sisters who died in childhood, and a
5 brother, Patrick Branwell, with whom they
6 were very close. The Bronte family lived a very
7 modest life and did not have the funds to send
8 the sisters to private schools, so they were
9 largely educated at home. Even at a young age,
10 the girls demonstrated a talent for narrative,
11 using their brother's twelve wooden toy
12 soldiers to create endless stories. They soon
13 began writing these stories down, creating epic
14 sagas about the fictional kingdoms of Glass
15 Town and the Empire of Agria.
16 The first work the sisters ever published,
17 appearing in 1846, was a joint collection of
18 poems entitled *Poems* by Currer, Ellis, and
19 Acton Bell. The sisters were forced to employ
20 these quasi-masculine pseudonyms because
21 the publishing company was worried that
22 poetry written by female authors simply
23 wouldn't sell. The sisters selected names that
24 would match their own initials so they could
25 reserve at least some ownership of the text.
26 In 1847, all three sisters published what
27 would come to be their most famous novels:
28 Charlotte's *Jane Eyre*, Emily's *Wuthering*
29 *Heights*, and Anne's *Agnes Grey*. Though
30 originally published under the same
31 pseudonyms, Charlotte and Emily Bronte
32 ended their anonymity when they travelled to
33 London to prove to their publisher that they
34 were indeed independent authors (a rumor
35 had started that "Ellis Bell" was in fact the
36 author of all three novels) and also female.
37 Though their gender had originally been feared
38 as a potential detriment to their novels'
39 success, this never came to pass; *Jane Eyre* and
40 *Wuthering Heights* were wildly successful and
41 remain popular literature today.

Go on to the next page ➡

25. The primary purpose of the passage is to
    (A) discuss the development of female authorship.
    (B) explain the origins of pseudonyms.
    (C) compare the careers of Charlotte, Emily, and Anne Bronte.
    (D) provide the history of three famous literary sisters.

26. In line 38, the word "detriment" most nearly means
    (A) boost.
    (B) hindrance.
    (C) fluke.
    (D) foreshadowing.

27. You would most likely expect to find this passage in
    (A) a piece in a literary history magazine.
    (B) an article in a scientific journal.
    (C) a blog post about different ways to use pseudonyms.
    (D) an advertisement for creative writing classes.

28. In the second paragraph (lines 16-25), the author implies that
    (A) the Bronte sisters stylistically preferred their pseudonyms to their given names.
    (B) publishing under a pseudonym was very fashionable in the 19th century.
    (C) Currer, Acton, and Ellis Bell helped the Bronte sisters write the poems.
    (D) the Bronte sisters were reluctant to publish anonymously.

29. The tone of the final paragraph could best be described as
    (A) triumphant.
    (B) critical.
    (C) timid.
    (D) perplexed.

30. Based on information given in the first paragraph, it can be inferred that
    (A) the Bronte sisters possessed enough talent to overcome their lack of formal education.
    (B) it was typical not to educate young girls during this time period.
    (C) Patrick Branwell didn't play with his toy soldiers.
    (D) the Bronte sisters' parents frowned upon their narrative exploits.

Go on to the next page ➡

Questions 31–36

1 Hard as it is to believe, it was once
2 standard public health policy to isolate those
3 who were sick with infectious disease in
4 isolation hospitals until they were no longer ill.
5 Whereas nowadays doctors realize that
6 isolation is only necessary in the cases of
7 extremely infectious diseases and only for
8 short periods of time, doctors in the early
9 twentieth century thought that isolation was
10 the most effective way to prevent the spread of
11 nearly all diseases. Public health officials ran
12 into a problem, however, when they discovered
13 that there could be apparently healthy people
14 carrying the bacteria of deadly diseases inside
15 their bodies. The problem is well-illustrated by
16 the story of Typhoid Mary.
17 Mary Mallon, aka "Typhoid Mary," was
18 the first known healthy carrier of typhoid fever.
19 Mary worked as a cook in the homes of wealthy
20 New Yorkers in the early 20th century. New
21 York public health officials traced several
22 outbreaks of typhoid fever to her cooking. The
23 officials determined that Mary transferred
24 typhoid bacteria from her unwashed hands to
25 the food she served the families. Laboratory
26 tests confirmed that Mary was playing host to
27 billions of typhoid bacteria, even though she
28 claimed to have never suffered from the
29 disease herself.
30 Once public health officials had located
31 Mary, they had to decide what to do with her.
32 Ultimately, the officials decided that Mary was
33 too dangerous to be allowed to roam freely,
34 particularly since she adamantly believed that
35 she was not a typhoid carrier and vowed to
36 continue cooking. The officials forcibly isolated
37 her in a one-room bungalow on North Brother
38 Island for nearly three decades until her death
39 in 1938. Her only companion was a small dog,
40 and journalists who came to interview her (for
41 by that point "Typhoid Mary" had become a
42 minor celebrity) were not even allowed to
43 accept a glass of water from her for fear of
44 contagion.
45 Such procedures seem unreasonably
46 draconian nowadays; it would be impossible to
47 restrict an individual's liberty to such an extent
48 in the present day. The case of Typhoid Mary
49 serves to show how quickly the relationship
50 between individual freedom and public health
51 has evolved in the last century.

Go on to the next page ➡

31. The main purpose of this passage is to
    (A) advocate for Typhoid Mary's immediate release from isolation.
    (B) discuss the case of Typhoid Mary as an example of changing public health policies.
    (C) explain the biological workings of typhoid fever.
    (D) demonstrate the importance of washing one's hands, especially in the foodservice industry.

32. In line 21, the word "traced" most nearly means
    (A) outlined.
    (B) connected.
    (C) drew.
    (D) discovered.

33. According to the passage, public health officials considered Mary Mallon a threat because
    (A) she might have children who would be typhoid carriers.
    (B) she refused to believe she was a typhoid carrier.
    (C) she routinely used disease-causing ingredients in her cooking.
    (D) she interacted primarily with wealthy people.

34. In the last paragraph (lines 45-51), it is implied that
    (A) public health standards have deteriorated since the time of Mary Mallon.
    (B) modern isolation facilities are much more pleasant than those which existed in the early 20th century.
    (C) Mary Mallon would have received different treatment if she had been discovered in the present day.
    (D) America will always value public health over individual freedom.

35. In line 46, the word "draconian" most nearly means
    (A) severe.
    (B) relaxed.
    (C) rational.
    (D) dangerous.

36. Which of the following sentences best describes the structure of the passage?
    (A) A debate between two ideas is presented, with evidence for each side.
    (B) A weak argument is followed by criticism, and rejection.
    (C) A specific historical example is discussed in relation to a broader problem.
    (D) A chronology of important events is presented, leaving the reader to draw conclusions.

STOP. Do not go on until told to do so.

SECTION 4

Mathematics Achievement

47 Questions **Time: 40 minutes**

Each question is followed by four suggested answers. Read each question and then decide which one of the four suggested answers is best.

Find the row of spaces on your answer document that has the same number as the question. In this row, mark the space having the same letter as the answer you have chosen. You may write in your test booklet.

SAMPLE QUESTION:

Sample Answer

Ⓐ ● Ⓒ Ⓓ

If $a = 3$, what is the value $a^2 + (3 \times 4) \div 6$?

(A) 3.5

(B) 11

(C) 14.5

(D) 20

The correct answer is 11, so circle B is darkened.

STOP. Do not go on until told to do so.

STOP

1. If $3 \geq Q + 1 > -2$, what could be a value of Q?
   (A) -3
   (B) -1
   (C) 3
   (D) 5

2. Which expression describes the values of x for which $|2x + 2| \leq 3$?
   (A) $x \leq \frac{1}{2}$
   (B) $-\frac{5}{2} \leq x$
   (C) $-\frac{5}{2} \leq x \leq \frac{1}{2}$
   (D) $x \leq -\frac{5}{2}$ or $x \geq \frac{1}{2}$

3. Mr. Jones has 8 white shirts, 4 black shirts, 5 blue shirts, and 3 yellow shirts. He chooses one shirt at random from his drawer, then puts it back and chooses another shirt at random. What is the probability that one shirt will be blue and that the other shirt will be white?
   (A) $\frac{1}{5} \times \frac{1}{8}$
   (B) $\frac{1}{4} \times \frac{2}{5}$
   (C) $\frac{7}{20}$
   (D) $\frac{13}{20}$

4. Which of the following expressions is equal to 5.214×10^8?
   (A) $5.21 \times 10^5 + 4 \times 10^3$
   (B) $(5.21 \times 10^5) \times (4 \times 10^3)$
   (C) $5.21 \times 10^8 + 4 \times 10^5$
   (D) $(5.21 \times 10^8) \times (4 \times 10^5)$

5. What is the value of the numerical expression $\sqrt{169 - 144}$?
   (A) 1
   (B) 2
   (C) 5
   (D) 10

6. Which of the following is equivalent to the expression $\frac{2^6 \times 4^2}{2^3 \times 2^2}$?
   (A) 2^3
   (B) 2^4
   (C) 2^5
   (D) 2^6

7. Mr. Gomez's 10 students take a quiz. The mean score is 8. If 2 more kids join the class and each receives a score of 9 on the quiz, what is the new mean score for the class?
   (A) $\frac{13}{6}$
   (B) $\frac{47}{6}$
   (C) 8
   (D) $\frac{49}{6}$

8. Sally and Jim both worked 8 hours yesterday and Jim makes half as much money per hour as Sally. If their total income was $120.00, what is Sally's hourly wage?
   (A) $5.00
   (B) $10.00
   (C) $15.00
   (D) $20.00

Go on to the next page ➡

9. Nathan needs to jump four long jumps that have an average length of 4.5 meters in order to qualify for the Olympics. His first three jumps had lengths of 3 meters, 4.5 meters, and 5 meters. What is the minimum length that he must jump on his fourth jump in order to qualify?

(A) 4 meters

(B) 4.5 meters

(C) 5 meters

(D) 5.5 meters

10. The number of frogs in various ponds is calculated and shown in the table below.

FROGS IN POND	
Number of Frogs	Number of Ponds Containing that Number of Frogs
0	2
20	4
40	3
60	6
80	9

Based on this data, what is the median number of frogs per pond?

(A) 20

(B) 40

(C) 60

(D) 80

11. Which expression is equivalent to the expression $\frac{z^3 2y^3 - 2z^3y^4}{z^2y^2}$?

(A) z^2

(B) $2zy - 2zy^2$

(C) $2z^2y - 2zy^2$

(D) $z^3y - 2z^2y^2$

Questions 12-13 refer to the stem-and-leaf plot below.

12. The stem-and-leaf plot shown represents exam scores for an algebra test.

Stem	Leaf
5	2 4 8
6	0 0 0 2
7	1 2 8
8	3 4 4 5
9	1 1 2 3 3

What is the mode exam score?

(A) 52

(B) 60

(C) 84

(D) 93

13. What is the median exam score?

(A) 60

(B) 72

(C) 78

(D) 83

14. A lock keypad requires the correct three digit code to activate it. You can use the numbers 0-9 for the code. The first and last numbers may be the same, but the middle number must be different than both the first and the last numbers. How many unique codes are possible for the keypad?

(A) 120

(B) 720

(C) 810

(D) 3,628,800

Go on to the next page ➡

15. Triangle ABC is shown. The length $\overline{BC}$ is 3 inches. The measure of ACB is 30°.

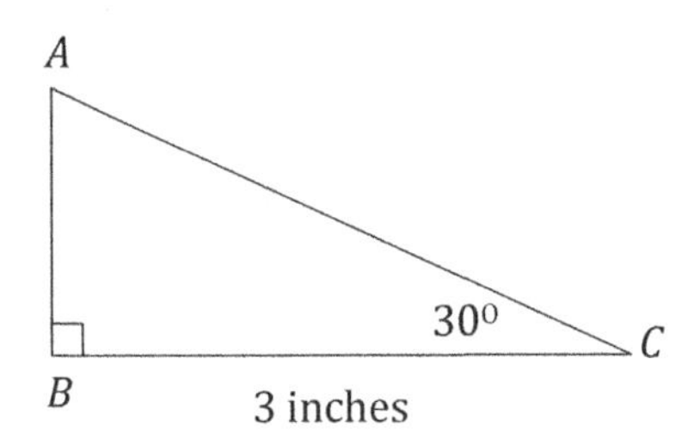

The value of which expression is equal to the length of side $\overline{AB}$?

(A) $\tan 30° \times 3$

(B) $\frac{\tan 30°}{3}$

(C) $\sin 30° \times 3$

(D) $\frac{\sin 30°}{3}$

16. The center of a circle is located at (0,-1). Point (2,2) is found on the circle's perimeter. What is the circle's radius?

(A) 2

(B) $\sqrt{5}$

(C) 3

(D) $\sqrt{13}$

17. What is the solution set for the expression $2y^2 + 162 = 0$?

(A) -9

(B) 9

(C) $9i$

(D) $\pm 9i$

18. Which expression is equivalent to the expression $\frac{1}{\sqrt{64x^{64}}}$?

(A) $\frac{x^{-32}}{8}$

(B) x^{-32}

(C) $2x^{32}$

(D) $(8x^8)^{-1}$

19. For what value(s) does $\frac{(y+2)(y-5)}{y(y^2-4)} = 0$?

(A) 5

(B) -2 and 2

(C) -2 and 5

(D) -2, 2 and 5

20. The surface area for the cone shown measures 24π. The formula for the surface area of a cone is $SA = \pi r^2 + r\pi s$, where r is the radius of the base of the cone and s is the cone's slant height.

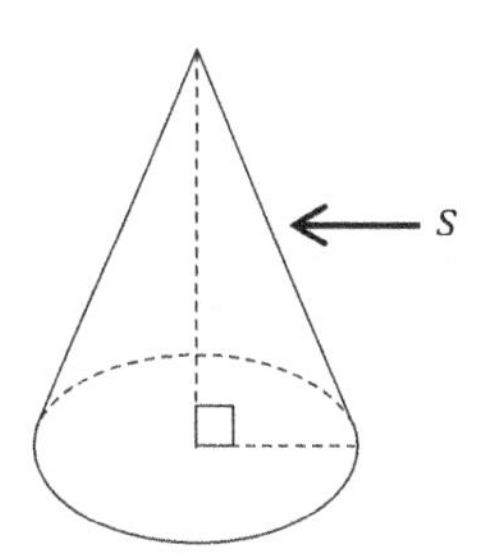

If the radius, r, is equal to 3, what is the slant height, s, of the cone?

(A) 2.5

(B) 5

(C) 25

(D) 12

Go on to the next page ➡

21. The following graph represents the solution set for which of following inequalities?

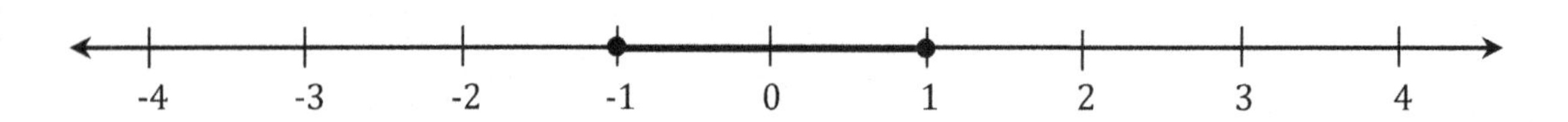

(A) $-1 \geq x + 3 \geq 1$
(B) $4 \geq 2x + 6 \geq 2$
(C) $8 \geq 2x + 6 \geq 4$
(D) $16 \geq 2x + 6 \geq 4$

Questions 22 to 23 are based on the box-and-whisker plot below.

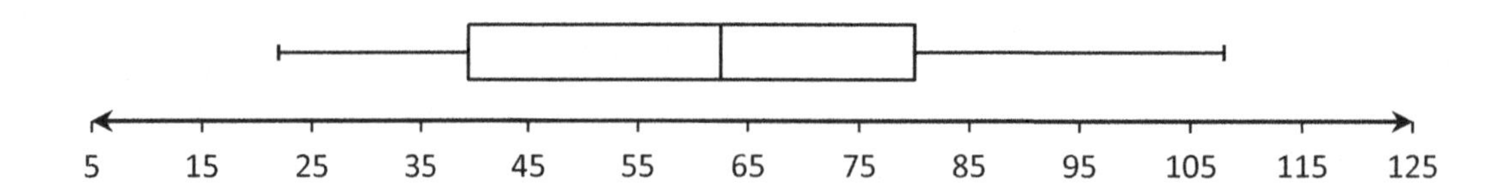

22. Which inequality best represents the median of the data found in the box-and-whisker plot above?
(A) $35 < median < 45$
(B) $55 < median < 65$
(C) $75 < median < 85$
(D) $95 < median < 115$

23. Which number falls within the third quartile of the box-and-whisker plot above?
(A) 35
(B) 45
(C) 55
(D) 75

Go on to the next page ➡

24. When measuring the volume of a cup of coffee, what is the best unit to use?

(A) milligram

(B) centimeter

(C) milliliter

(D) millisecond

25. Two similar triangles are shown below.

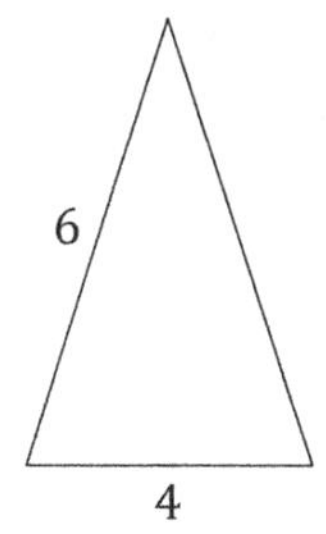

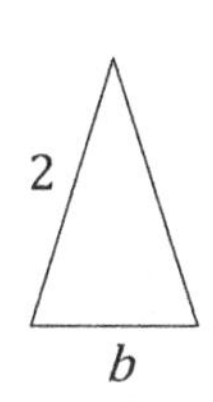

Note: Figures not drawn to scale.

What is the value of b?

(A) $\frac{2}{3}$

(B) 1

(C) $\frac{4}{3}$

(D) 4

26. George wants to determine the average number of children per family in his city. Which sample will provide him with the most reliable information about the average number of children per family in his city?

(A) the families that he knows on his city block

(B) the families that show up at a picnic in his city's park

(C) a random sample of the families that sign up for recreational sports in his city

(D) a random sample of all the families in his city

27. Which expression is equivalent to the expression $(3x + 3)(3x + 3)$?

(A) $9x^2 - 9$

(B) $9x^3 - 9$

(C) $9x^2 + 18x + 9$

(D) $9x^3 + 18x + 9$

28. Which expression is equivalent to the expression $(x - 2)(x^2 + 2x + 4)$?

(A) $x^2 - 4$

(B) $2x^2 - 4$

(C) $x^3 - 8$

(D) $x^3 + 8$

29. The graph of a line is shown.

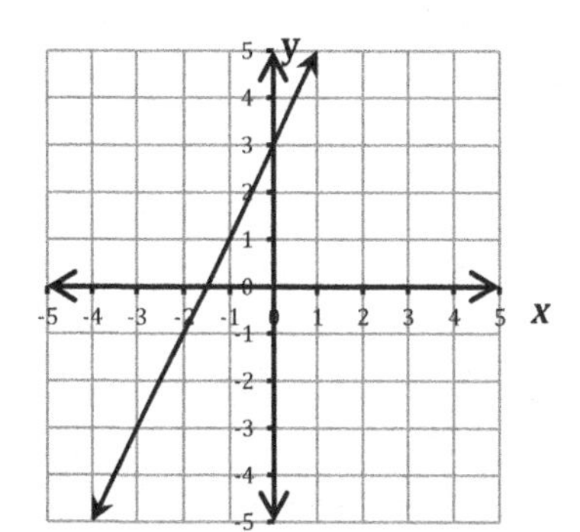

What is the slope of the line?

(A) -2

(B) -1

(C) 1

(D) 2

Go on to the next page ➡

30. The results of 10 Olympic scores are shown in a bar graph.

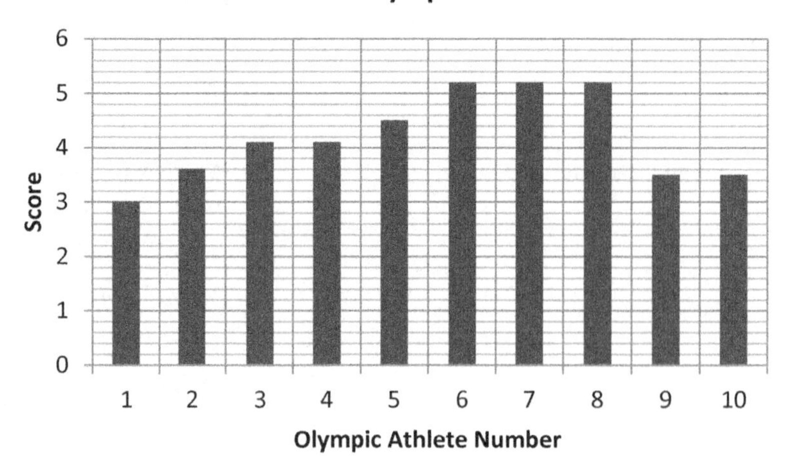

What is the mode of the scores?

(A) 1

(B) 3.5

(C) 4.1

(D) 5.2

---

31. A rectangle bisects two identical circles as shown.

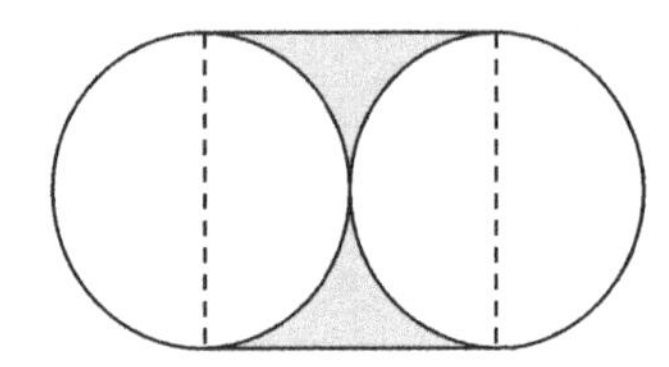

If the radius of the circles is 3, what is the area of the shaded space within the rectangle?

(A) $36 - \pi$

(B) $36 - 9\pi$

(C) $36 - \frac{9\pi}{2}$

(D) 36

32. A backpack contains 3 conch shells, 4 oyster shells, 6 snail shells, and 2 nassa shells. Joon randomly removes one shell from the backpack and leaves it by the sea. Joon's sister then randomly removes a shell from the backpack. If the shell Joon removed from the backpack is a conch shell, what is the probability that the shell his sister removed is a snail shell?

(A) $\frac{1}{7}$

(B) $\frac{1}{6}$

(C) $\frac{6}{15}$

(D) $\frac{3}{7}$

Go on to the next page ➡

33. Which value is equal to $3\frac{2}{9}$?

(A) $\frac{19}{6}$

(B) 3.3333333

(C) $3.\overline{2}$

(D) 3.2222

34. If $za + 2z = 4a + 8$ and $a \neq -2$, what is a possible value for z?

(A) -3

(B) 0

(C) 2

(D) 4

35. Abena has 8 kinds of ingredients and cooking a meal requires 4 different ingredients. If the order of the ingredients makes no difference to the meal, and Abena uses no more than the 4 ingredients required for each meal, how many different meals can Abena make?

(A) 8

(B) 32

(C) 70

(D) 1680

36. If a and d are prime numbers, what is the greatest common factor of $a\sqrt{81d}$, $27da$, and $18a$?

(A) $3a\sqrt{d}$

(B) $3ad$

(C) $9a\sqrt{d}$

(D) $9ad$

37. Factory A makes four times the waste of factory B. If the total waste from the two factories weighs 40 tons, how much waste was made by factory B?

(A) 4 tons

(B) 8 tons

(C) 16 tons

(D) 32 tons

38. Which expression represents an integer?

(A) 2π

(B) $\sqrt{16-4}$

(C) $\frac{3^{0.5}\times 3}{3^{-0.5}}$

(D) $\sqrt{-1}$

39. The area of each grid unit is 3 cm^2.

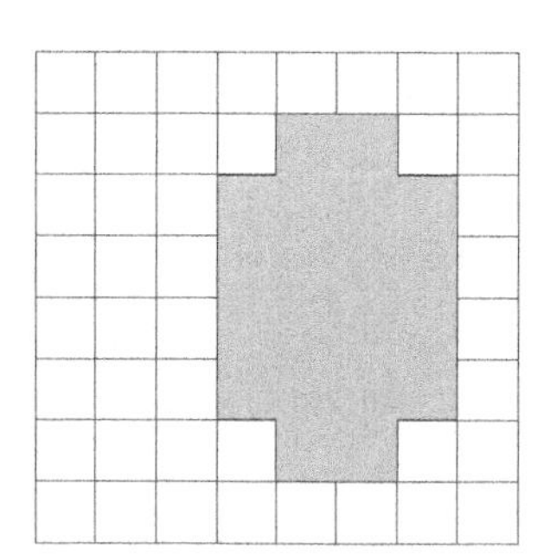

What is the area of the unshaded region?

(A) 20 cm^2

(B) 60 cm^2

(C) 64 cm^2

(D) 132 cm^2

Go on to the next page ➡

Questions 40 to 41 refer to the histogram below.

40. A histogram shows the height of the population in Greenville.

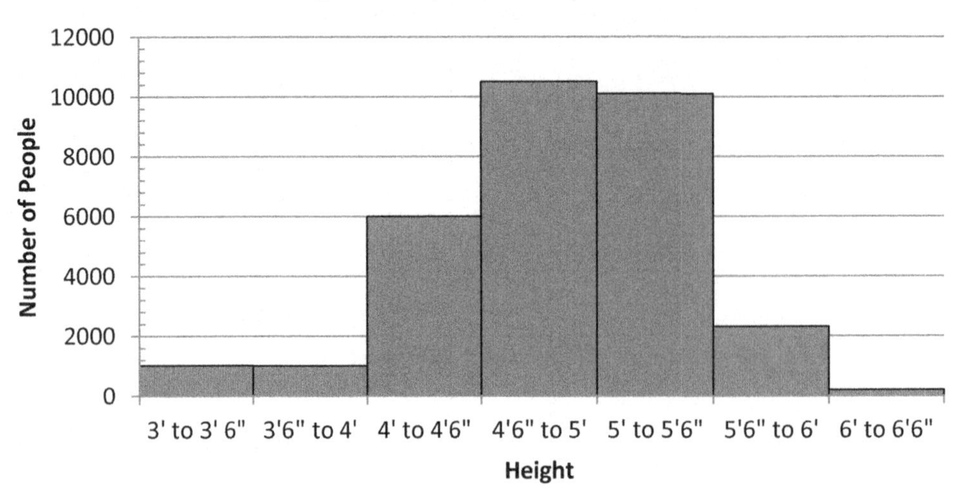

What is the range of the height of the population in Greenville?

(A) 3’

(B) 3’6”

(C) 4’6”

(D) 6’6”

41. What is the median height category of the population in Greenville?

(A) 4’to 4’6”

(B) 4’6” to 5’

(C) 5’ to 5’6”

(D) 5’6” to 6’

Go on to the next page ➡

42. The graph of a line is shown.

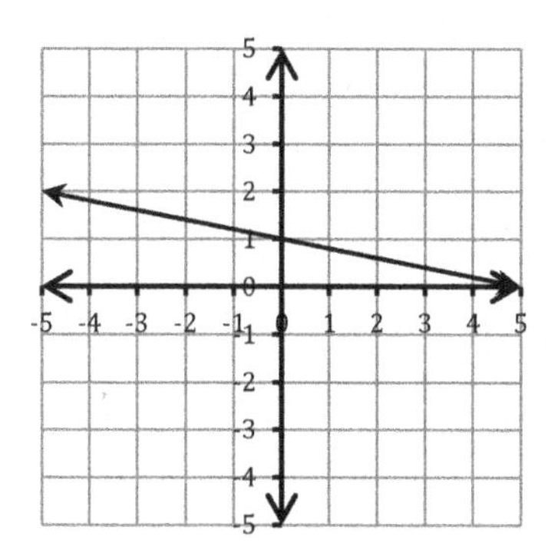

Which of the following could be the equation of a line that is perpendicular to this line?

(A) $y = -\frac{1}{5}x$

(B) $y = -\frac{1}{5}x + 1$

(C) $y = \frac{1}{5}x + 1$

(D) $y = 5x + 1$

43. Two lines bisect each other, forming two isosceles triangles.

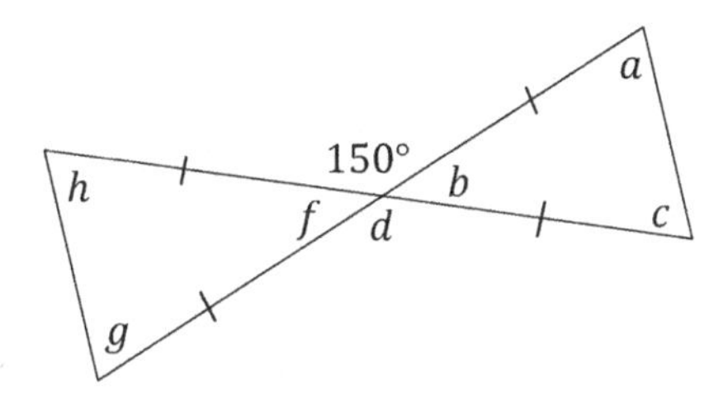

What is the value for angle h?

(A) 30°

(B) 75°

(C) 90°

(D) 150°

44. A cylinder is shown below. The formula for the volume of a cylinder is $V = r^2 h\pi$, where r is the cylinder's radius and h is the cylinder's height.

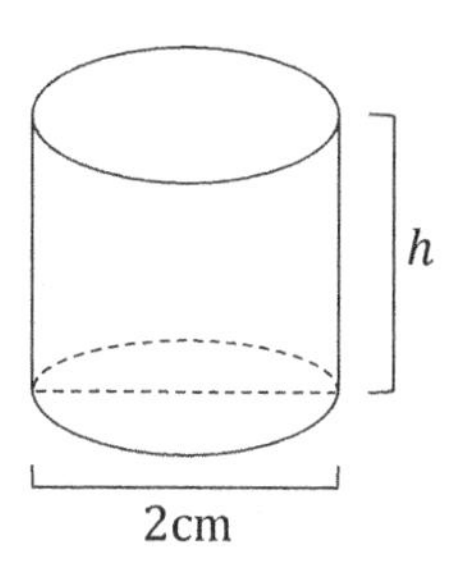

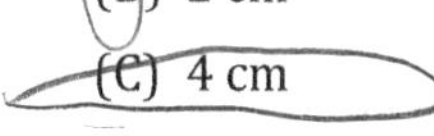

If the cylinder has a diameter of 2 cm and a volume of 4π cm^3, what is its height?

(A) 1 cm

(B) 2 cm

(C) 4 cm

(D) 8 cm

45. Points $(-3,-2)$, $(-1,1)$, and $(2,-2)$ form three points of a parallelogram. What are the coordinates of the remaining point?

(A) $(-4,1)$

(B) $(-2,2)$

(C) $(2,1)$

(D) $(4,1)$

Go on to the next page ➡

46. A sphere is placed in a cube. The formula used to find the volume of a sphere is $V = \frac{4}{3}\pi r^3$, where r is the radius of the sphere. The cube has a volume of 8 cm^3 and the length of one side of the cube is equal to the diameter of the sphere.

    What is the volume of the empty space remaining in the cube after the sphere is placed in the cube?

    (A) $8 - \frac{32}{3}\pi$

    (B) $8 - \frac{4}{3}\pi$

    (C) $\frac{4}{3}\pi$

    (D) $\frac{32}{3}\pi$

47. What is the result of the expression $\begin{bmatrix} -1 & 3 \\ 5 & 1 \end{bmatrix} - \begin{bmatrix} 2 & 3 \\ 2 & 4 \end{bmatrix}$?

    (A) $\begin{bmatrix} -3 & 0 \\ 3 & -3 \end{bmatrix}$

    (B) $\begin{bmatrix} 2 & 3 \\ 2 & 4 \end{bmatrix}$

    (C) $\begin{bmatrix} -1 & 3 \\ 5 & 1 \end{bmatrix}$

    (D) $\begin{bmatrix} 4 & 9 \\ 12 & 19 \end{bmatrix}$

STOP. Do not go on until told to do so.

STOP

Essay Topic Sheet

The directions for the Essay portion of the ISEE are printed in the box below. Use the pre-lined pages on pages 86-87 for this part of the Practice Test.

You will have 30 minutes to plan and write an essay on the topic printed on the other side of this page. **Do not write on another topic. An essay on another topic is not acceptable.**

The essay is designed to give you an opportunity to show how well you can write. You should try to express your thoughts clearly. How well you write is much more important than how much you write, but you need to say enough for a reader to understand what you mean.

You will probably want to write more than a short paragraph. You should also be aware that a copy of your essay will be sent to each school that will be receiving your test results. You are to write only in the appropriate section of the answer sheet. Please write or print so that your writing may be read by someone who is not familiar with your handwriting.

You may make notes and plan your essay on the reverse side of the page. Allow enough time to copy the final form onto your answer sheet. You must copy the essay topic onto your answer sheet, on page 86, in the box provided.

Please remember to write only the final draft of the essay on pages 86-87 of your answer sheet and to write it in blue or black pen. Again, you may use cursive writing or you may print. Only pages 86-87 will be sent to the schools.

Directions continue on the next page.

REMINDER: Please write this essay topic on the first few lines of the first page of your essay sheet.

Essay Topic

What piece of modern technology do you think has most improved your own life? Explain why it has been important to you.

- Only write on this essay question
- Only pages 86 and 87 will be sent to the schools
- Only write in blue or black pen

NOTES

ANSWER KEYS

CHAPTER 4

PRACTICE TEST 1

UPPER LEVEL

SECTION 1 – VERBAL REASONING (PAGES 40-44)

1. A
2. D
3. A
4. C
5. B
6. D
7. C
8. B
9. A
10. B
11. C
12. D
13. C
14. D
15. B
16. A
17. B
18. D
19. B
20. C
21. D
22. C
23. D
24. B
25. D
26. B
27. D
28. C
29. B
30. D
31. A
32. C
33. C
34. B
35. B
36. A
37. D
38. A
39. B
40. C

SECTION 2 – QUANTITATIVE REASONING (PAGES 47-55)

1. B
2. C
3. A
4. D
5. B
6. A
7. C
8. D
9. A
10. C
11. D
12. C
13. B
14. A
15. C
16. D
17. A
18. B
19. B
20. B
21. A
22. D
23. B
24. A
25. A
26. B
27. C
28. B
29. C
30. C
31. A
32. A
33. A
34. B
35. B
36. A
37. C

SECTION 3 – READING COMPREHENSION (PAGES 57-68)

1. C
2. A
3. B
4. C
5. D
6. D
7. A
8. C
9. C
10. B
11. A
12. B
13. C
14. D
15. B
16. D
17. B
18. C
19. C
20. D
21. D
22. C
23. C
24. A
25. A
26. B
27. D
28. A
29. D
30. C
31. C
32. C
33. A
34. B
35. A
36. C

SECTION 4 – MATHEMATICS ACHIEVEMENT (PAGES 70-78)

1. A
2. C
3. C
4. A
5. B
6. B
7. B
8. C
9. D
10. C
11. A
12. D
13. D
14. B
15. D
16. A
17. C
18. A
19. C
20. C
21. D
22. B
23. C
24. A
25. B
26. B
27. C
28. B
29. B
30. C
31. C
32. D
33. C
34. B
35. C
36. D
37. C
38. C
39. D
40. A
41. C
42. C
43. B
44. D
45. A
46. D
47. C

SCORING YOUR TEST

On the ISEE, you receive one point for every question you answered correctly, and you receive no points for questions you answered incorrectly or skipped. In each section, the ISEE also includes 5 or 6 experimental questions that do not count towards your score. You won't be told which questions are unscored, and for this reason, these practice tests do not have specific questions marked as experimental. This also means that it isn't possible to determine an exact score for each section of these practice tests, but you can estimate your score using the procedures below.

To estimate your **raw score** for your practice test, first count up the number of questions you answered correctly in each section. Then, follow the table below to subtract 5 or 6 points for each section, accounting for the experimental questions that would not be scored on your actual ISEE exam.

MY RAW SCORE			
Section	**# of Questions Correct**		**Raw Score**
Verbal Reasoning		– 5 =	
Quantitative Reasoning		– 5 =	
Reading Comprehension		– 6 =	
Mathematics Achievement		– 5 =	

SCALED SCORE

Once you have found your raw score, convert it into an approximate **scaled score** using the scoring charts that follow. These charts provide an estimated range for your ISEE scaled score based on your performance on this practice test. Keep in mind that this estimate may differ slightly from your scaled score when you take your actual ISEE exam, depending on the ISEE's specific scaling for that exam and any differences in your own test-taking process.

UPPER LEVEL SCALED SCORE RANGES				
Raw Score	**Verbal Reasoning**	**Quantitative Reasoning**	**Reading Comprehension**	**Mathematics Achievement**
42				920 – 950
41				920 – 950
40				915 – 945
39				915 – 945
38				910 – 940
37				910 – 935
36				905 – 935
35	910 – 940			900 – 930
34	910 – 940			900 – 930
33	905 – 935			895 – 925
32	905 – 935	915 – 945		895 – 925
31	900 – 930	910 – 940		890 – 920
30	900 – 930	910 – 940	910 – 940	890 – 920
29	895 – 925	905 – 935	905 – 935	885 – 915
28	890 – 920	900 – 930	900 – 930	880 – 910
27	890 – 920	900 – 930	900 – 930	880 – 910
26	885 – 915	895 – 925	895 – 925	875 – 905
25	885 – 910	890 – 920	890 – 920	875 – 905
24	880 – 910	890 – 920	885 – 915	870 – 900
23	875 – 905	885 – 915	885 – 915	870 – 900
22	875 – 905	880 – 910	880 – 910	865 – 895
21	870 – 900	880 – 910	875 – 905	865 – 895
20	870 – 900	875 – 905	870 – 900	860 – 890

19	865 – 895	870 – 900	870 – 900	860 – 890
18	860 – 890	870 – 900	865 – 895	855 – 885
17	860 – 890	865 – 895	860 – 890	855 – 885
16	855 – 885	860 – 890	855 – 885	850 – 880
15	850 – 880	860 – 890	855 – 885	845 – 875
14	850 – 880	855 – 885	850 – 880	845 – 875
13	845 – 875	850 – 880	845 – 875	840 – 870
12	845 – 875	845 – 875	840 – 870	840 – 870
11	840 – 870	845 – 875	840 – 870	835 – 865
10	840 – 870	840 – 870	835 – 865	835 – 865
9	835 – 865	835 – 865	830 – 860	830 – 860
8	835 – 865	835 – 865	825 – 855	830 – 860
7	830 – 860	830 – 860	825 – 855	825 – 855
6	825 – 855	825 – 855	820 – 850	825 – 855
5	825 – 855	825 – 855	815 – 845	820 – 850
4	820 – 850	820 – 850	810 – 840	820 – 850
3	815 – 845	815 – 845	810 – 840	815 – 845
2	815 – 845	815 – 845	805 – 835	810 – 840
1	810 – 840	810 – 840	800 – 830	810 – 840
0	805 – 840	805 – 835	795 – 825	805 – 835

PERCENTILE

When you take your actual ISEE exam, you will receive a **percentile** ranking comparing your performance against the performance of other students in the same grade who have taken the ISEE that year. For example, a percentile of 62 means that you scored higher than 62% of other ISEE test-takers applying to the same grade. Because your percentile ranking shows how well you performed according to your own grade level, these rankings are frequently given high consideration by admissions offices.

The following charts provide an estimate of your ISEE percentile rankings for this practice test, compared against other students applying to the same grade. For example, if you are scoring at or above the 75th percentile, you are scoring higher than 75% of other ISEE test-takers applying to the same grade. Keep in mind that these percentiles are estimates only, and your actual ISEE percentile will depend on the specific group of students taking the exam in your year.

UPPER LEVEL VERBAL REASONING PERCENTILES			
Grade Applying To	**75th percentile**	**50th percentile**	**25th percentile**
Grade 9	893	879	866
Grade 10	899	883	867
Grade 11	902	886	869
Grade 12	898	881	863

UPPER LEVEL QUANTITATIVE REASONING PERCENTILES			
Grade Applying To	**75th percentile**	**50th percentile**	**25th percentile**
Grade 9	892	878	866
Grade 10	897	882	868
Grade 11	901	885	870
Grade 12	897	884	872

UPPER LEVEL READING COMPREHENSION PERCENTILES			
Grade Applying To	**75th percentile**	**50th percentile**	**25th percentile**
Grade 9	897	880	865
Grade 10	902	886	868
Grade 11	903	889	868
Grade 12	899	880	862

UPPER LEVEL MATHEMATICS ACHIEVEMENT PERCENTILES			
Grade Applying To	**75th percentile**	**50th percentile**	**25th percentile**
Grade 9	894	882	869
Grade 10	900	886	871
Grade 11	905	890	875
Grade 12	903	889	875

STANINE

When you receive the score report for your actual ISEE exam, your percentile score will also be broken down into a **stanine**. A stanine is a number from 1-9 obtained by dividing the entire range of students' scores into 9 segments, as shown in the table below:

PERCENTILE RANK	STANINE
1 – 3	1
4 – 10	2
11 – 22	3
23 – 39	4

40 – 59	5
60 – 76	6
77 – 88	7
89 – 95	8
96 – 99	9

Although it isn't possible to calculate your exact stanine from this practice test, you can estimate a stanine score range by looking at your estimated percentile score on each section. For example, if you scored between the 50th and 75th percentile in one of your test sections, your stanine score would be between 5 and 6.

PRACTICE TEST 2

UPPER LEVEL

SECTION 1 – VERBAL REASONING (PAGES 90-94)

1. A	6. D	11. A	16. A	21. A	26. D	31. A	36. C
2. D	7. C	12. D	17. C	22. B	27. B	32. D	37. A
3. D	8. D	13. C	18. B	23. C	28. C	33. B	38. A
4. D	9. D	14. C	19. B	24. C	29. B	34. C	39. B
5. B	10. A	15. B	20. A	25. C	30. D	35. B	40. D

SECTION 2 – QUANTITATIVE REASONING (PAGES 97-104)

1. A	6. B	11. C	16. D	21. B	26. B	31. B	36. C
2. A	7. C	12. B	17. C	22. B	27. D	32. C	37. B
3. B	8. B	13. B	18. B	23. A	28. B	33. B	
4. C	9. A	14. C	19. A	24. A	29. C	34. D	
5. D	10. A	15. D	20. D	25. D	30. A	35. C	

SECTION 3 – READING COMPREHENSION (PAGES 106-117)

1. C	6. C	11. B	16. B	21. A	26. B	31. B	36. C
2. A	7. C	12. B	17. D	22. A	27. A	32. B	
3. A	8. C	13. D	18. C	23. B	28. D	33. B	
4. B	9. D	14. D	19. D	24. A	29. A	34. C	
5. C	10. A	15. A	20. D	25. D	30. A	35. A	

SECTION 4 – MATHEMATICS ACHIEVEMENT (PAGES 119-128)

1. B	7. D	13. C	19. C	25. C	31. B	37. B	43. B
2. C	8. B	14. C	20. B	26. D	32. D	38. C	44. C
3. B	9. D	15. A	21. C	27. C	33. C	39. D	45. D
4. C	10. C	16. D	22. B	28. C	34. D	40. B	46. B
5. C	11. B	17. D	23. D	29. D	35. C	41. B	47. A
6. C	12. B	18. A	24. C	30. D	36. C	42. D	

SCORING YOUR TEST

On the ISEE, you receive one point for every question you answered correctly, and you receive no points for questions you answered incorrectly or skipped. In each section, the ISEE also includes 5 or 6 experimental questions that do not count towards your score. You won't be told which questions are unscored, and for this reason, these practice tests do not have specific questions marked as experimental. This also means that it isn't possible to determine an exact score for each section of these practice tests, but you can estimate your score using the procedures below.

To estimate your **raw score** for your practice test, first count up the number of questions you answered correctly in each section. Then, follow the table below to subtract 5 or 6 points for each section, accounting for the experimental questions that would not be scored on your actual ISEE exam.

MY RAW SCORE			
Section	**# of Questions Correct**		**Raw Score**
Verbal Reasoning		− 5 =	
Quantitative Reasoning		− 5 =	
Reading Comprehension		− 6 =	
Mathematics Achievement		− 5 =	

SCALED SCORE

Once you have found your raw score, convert it into an approximate **scaled score** using the scoring charts that follow. These charts provide an estimated range for your ISEE scaled score based on your performance on this practice test. Keep in mind that this estimate may differ slightly from your scaled score when you take your actual ISEE exam, depending on the ISEE's specific scaling for that exam and any differences in your own test-taking process.

UPPER LEVEL SCALED SCORE RANGES				
Raw Score	Verbal Reasoning	Quantitative Reasoning	Reading Comprehension	Mathematics Achievement
42				920 – 950
41				920 – 950
40				915 – 945
39				915 – 945
38				910 – 940
37				910 – 935
36				905 – 935
35	910 – 940			900 – 930
34	910 – 940			900 – 930
33	905 – 935			895 – 925
32	905 – 935	915 – 945		895 – 925
31	900 – 930	910 – 940		890 – 920
30	900 – 930	910 – 940	910 – 940	890 – 920
29	895 – 925	905 – 935	905 – 935	885 – 915
28	890 – 920	900 – 930	900 – 930	880 – 910
27	890 – 920	900 – 930	900 – 930	880 – 910
26	885 – 915	895 – 925	895 – 925	875 – 905
25	885 – 910	890 – 920	890 – 920	875 – 905
24	880 – 910	890 – 920	885 – 915	870 – 900
23	875 – 905	885 – 915	885 – 915	870 – 900
22	875 – 905	880 – 910	880 – 910	865 – 895
21	870 – 900	880 – 910	875 – 905	865 – 895
20	870 – 900	875 – 905	870 – 900	860 – 890

19	865 – 895	870 – 900	870 – 900	860 – 890
18	860 – 890	870 – 900	865 – 895	855 – 885
17	860 – 890	865 – 895	860 – 890	855 – 885
16	855 – 885	860 – 890	855 – 885	850 – 880
15	850 – 880	860 – 890	855 – 885	845 – 875
14	850 – 880	855 – 885	850 – 880	845 – 875
13	845 – 875	850 – 880	845 – 875	840 – 870
12	845 – 875	845 – 875	840 – 870	840 – 870
11	840 – 870	845 – 875	840 – 870	835 – 865
10	840 – 870	840 – 870	835 – 865	835 – 865
9	835 – 865	835 – 865	830 – 860	830 – 860
8	835 – 865	835 – 865	825 – 855	830 – 860
7	830 – 860	830 – 860	825 – 855	825 – 855
6	825 – 855	825 – 855	820 – 850	825 – 855
5	825 – 855	825 – 855	815 – 845	820 – 850
4	820 – 850	820 – 850	810 – 840	820 – 850
3	815 – 845	815 – 845	810 – 840	815 – 845
2	815 – 845	815 – 845	805 – 835	810 – 840
1	810 – 840	810 – 840	800 – 830	810 – 840
0	805 – 840	805 – 835	795 – 825	805 – 835

PERCENTILE

When you take your actual ISEE exam, you will receive a **percentile** ranking comparing your performance against the performance of other students in the same grade who have taken the ISEE that year. For example, a percentile of 62 means that you scored higher than 62% of other ISEE test-takers applying to the same grade. Because your percentile ranking shows how well you performed according to your own grade level, these rankings are frequently given high consideration by admissions offices.

The following charts provide an estimate of your ISEE percentile rankings for this practice test, compared against other students applying to the same grade. For example, if you are scoring at or above the 75th percentile, you are scoring higher than 75% of other ISEE test-takers applying to the same grade. Keep in mind that these percentiles are estimates only, and your actual ISEE percentile will depend on the specific group of students taking the exam in your year.

UPPER LEVEL VERBAL REASONING PERCENTILES			
Grade Applying To	**75th percentile**	**50th percentile**	**25th percentile**
Grade 9	893	879	866
Grade 10	899	883	867
Grade 11	902	886	869
Grade 12	898	881	863

UPPER LEVEL QUANTITATIVE REASONING PERCENTILES			
Grade Applying To	**75th percentile**	**50th percentile**	**25th percentile**
Grade 9	892	878	866
Grade 10	897	882	868
Grade 11	901	885	870
Grade 12	897	884	872

UPPER LEVEL READING COMPREHENSION PERCENTILES			
Grade Applying To	**75th percentile**	**50th percentile**	**25th percentile**
Grade 9	897	880	865
Grade 10	902	886	868
Grade 11	903	889	868
Grade 12	899	880	862

UPPER LEVEL MATHEMATICS ACHIEVEMENT PERCENTILES			
Grade Applying To	**75th percentile**	**50th percentile**	**25th percentile**
Grade 9	894	882	869
Grade 10	900	886	871
Grade 11	905	890	875
Grade 12	903	889	875

STANINE

When you receive the score report for your actual ISEE exam, your percentile score will also be broken down into a **stanine**. A stanine is a number from 1-9 obtained by dividing the entire range of students' scores into 9 segments, as shown in the table below:

PERCENTILE RANK	STANINE
1 – 3	1
4 – 10	2
11 – 22	3
23 – 39	4

40 – 59	5
60 – 76	6
77 – 88	7
89 – 95	8
96 – 99	9

Although it isn't possible to calculate your exact stanine from this practice test, you can estimate a stanine score range by looking at your estimated percentile score on each section. For example, if you scored between the 50th and 75th percentile in one of your test sections, your stanine score would be between 5 and 6.

Made in the USA
Las Vegas, NV
24 March 2022